Why Sunday Matters

Why Sunday Matters

The Lord's Day in Contemporary Christian Life

JOSHUA J. WHITFIELD

CASCADE *Books* • Eugene, Oregon

WHY SUNDAY MATTERS
The Lord's Day in Contemporary Christian Life

Copyright © 2024 Joshua J. Whitfield. All rights reserved. Except for brief quotations in critical publications or reviews, no part of this book may be reproduced in any manner without prior written permission from the publisher. Write: Permissions, Wipf and Stock Publishers, 199 W. 8th Ave., Suite 3, Eugene, OR 97401.

Cascade Books
An Imprint of Wipf and Stock Publishers
199 W. 8th Ave., Suite 3
Eugene, OR 97401

www.wipfandstock.com

PAPERBACK ISBN: 979-8-3852-2187-5
HARDCOVER ISBN: 979-8-3852-2188-2
EBOOK ISBN: 979-8-3852-2189-9

Cataloguing-in-Publication data:

Names: Whitfield, Joshua Jair, author.
Title: Why sunday matters : the lord's day in contemporary christian life / Joshua J. Whitfield.
Description: Eugene, OR : Cascade Books, 2024 | Includes bibliographical references and index.
Identifiers: ISBN 979-8-3852-2187-5 (paperback) | ISBN 979-8-3852-2188-2 (hardcover) | ISBN 979-8-3852-2189-9 (ebook)
Subjects: LCSH: Sabbath. | Sunday.
Classification: BV111 .W45 2024 (paperback) | BV111 .W45 (ebook)

VERSION NUMBER 10/14/24

Scripture texts in this work are taken from the *New American Bible, revised edition* © 2010, 1991, 1986, 1970 Confraternity of Christian Doctrine, Washington, D.C. and are used by permission of the copyright owner. All Rights Reserved. No part of the New American Bible may be reproduced in any form without permission in writing from the copyright owner.

Contents

Prologue | vii
1 The Sunday Christ | 1
2 The Religion of Sports | 15
3 Pure Play | 31
4 The Poor and Work, or Why We Cannot See the Sabbath | 45
5 Discerning the Body and Seeing the Sabbath | 64
6 The Devil in the Garden | 82
7 Digital Temporality and the Sabbath | 100
Epilogue | 114
Bibliography | 117

Prologue

THIS BOOK IS ABOUT the Lord's Day, Sunday. An extended meditation, first and briefly, upon the meaning of the day itself, it has ended up mostly an examination (at times searingly penitential) of those areas and elements in our lives wherein and by which we lose sight of, forget, and fail to welcome Sunday. It is an examination of something missing from our lives—and not only those portions of our lives we cordon off as Christian or Catholic—that, however unacknowledged, marks a profound spiritual and human deficiency constituting a profound spiritual and human tragedy. This book is about things we barely think about but should. It's a book about some of the deeper causes of our current restlessness.

This book is about the Sabbath, which believers in Jesus welcome *in him*—at all times, of course, but especially on Sunday, the Lord's Day. I attended recently, with my bishop, the Kabbalat Shabbat, a Jewish liturgy welcoming the Sabbath, at a local conservative synagogue. What I experienced there was something akin to my experience writing this book; it may be like your experience reading it. For it was an experience of the familiar as unfamiliar. It was to pray the Psalms with a mysterious, unsettled distance. Still inviting, as instinctive allegories began to echo at a whisper, it was to hear within them a beautiful, unusual resonance they always obviously possessed but which felt new and which begged the soul to look, to search. Singing songs of God's rest, of his voice upon the waters, kindling fire, singing the ancient kabbalistic hymn *L'kha dodi*, as we turned to the door to welcome the Sabbath—"Welcome

Prologue

Shabbat the Bride, Queen of our days"—all of it played, as Paul Griffiths recently put it, like a fugue deepening my unfamiliarity with the familiar. There I rediscovered Sabbath in a liturgy more primitive, yet as alive, as my own.[1] To grasp, to feel, to rediscover the Lord welcomed in time and in place—a synagogue at Friday's dusk—was to be brought back to a wisdom that is still meant for Christians, wisdom similarly timebound and local. It was to be reminded of a weekly gift and mystery most of us no longer think about: the Christian practice of Sunday.

This book, therefore, begins a rediscovery. It is only a beginning. Why does Sunday matter? How should Christians—Catholic Christians especially—think about Sunday and live under its blessings? And what prevents us from doing so? These are the questions this small book asks; the answers you can judge for yourself. If, however, this book succeeds or fails, it will not be due to any answers it pretends to offer but to the quality of its assertion that Sunday still matters, that being faithful to the Lord's Day remains a grave spiritual necessity.

But before we proceed, I think it helpful to alert the reader to something and also to admit something: the latter, a fault of mine I've not been able to shake as a thinker and writer, and the former something personal. First: I am a married Catholic priest, a convert from Anglicanism. Thus, when I refer to my children, I beg Catholic readers not to be scandalized or distracted. Second: to quote an old parishioner of mine, I quote a lot of "dead people." I do. To be fair, however, I quote a lot of living people too. And while I admit this may count against me as a writer, or even intellectually, I do so because I consider the practice of the faith, and life generally, a matter for conversation and at times argument. That is, I think it belongs to the tradition to mark, learn, and share what others have thought and said, and then to speak with those other voices in the common search for truth. Too many to quote have said exactly that, and I believe them all. In any case, quoting as many people as I do at least helps me avoid being so foolish as to pretend I'm offering anything *de novo*.

1. Griffiths, *Israel*.

Prologue

As always, I am grateful to my bishops, Bishop Edward Burns and Bishop Greg Kelly, and my brother priests and deacons. Their welcome and continued inspiration is grace. I am grateful to my parish, Saint Rita Catholic Community in Dallas, Texas, a beautiful community in which to live out my priesthood. I'm also thankful to all those friends who've given me hospitality all over the world, but especially to the Cistercians of Our Lady of Dallas and to Thom and Jan Schliem, without whom this book would not have been written. I'm deeply thankful also to the many friends I burdened with reading repeated drafts of this book. You have saved me much embarrassment. I'm uniquely grateful as well to my friend and colleague Grady Baldock, for driving late one night out into the wilds of Texas to bring me a working computer. He is the greatest IT guy on earth, or at least I think so. It was a kindness I'll not forget.

And finally, most of all, I'm grateful to my wife Alli and to our five children. They give much to the Church. They enrich my priesthood. I am blessed to be a domestic church with them—so beautiful, so noisy, so funny and full of joy. Graces upon graces, I am indeed a blessed and thankful father in so many ways, and for that I dedicate this book to them. May we find the Sabbath together.

—Joshua J. Whitfield
Epiphany 2024

1

The Sunday Christ

> Come to me, all you who labor and are burdened, and I
> will give you rest.
>
> —MATTHEW 11:28

IT'S CALLED THE SUNDAY Christ—in German, *Sontagchristus*, in French, *Christ du Dimanche*, in Italian, *Cristo della Domenica*.[1] A niche artifact of medieval devotion, only a handful of examples remain. Faded on the crumbling walls of old churches, it is a kind of art almost entirely lost to believers today. For many years, in fact, the image was misinterpreted. No one knew what it meant, so different was medieval piety and morality from ours.

The image is of Jesus, scourged and bloodied. It is like the Man of Sorrows, that better known image of the suffering Christ surrounded by the implements of his torture—hammers and nails, the lance, the crown of thorns, the dice. But the Sunday Christ is different. In place of the instruments of the passion, the bloodied Christ is surrounded instead by more ordinary objects, at least to medieval eyes: instead of a lance, a fisherman's hook; instead of

1. Reiss, *Sunday Christ*, 2.

Why Sunday Matters

dice, a lute or playing cards; instead of hammers and nails, a pair of tailor's scissors and a weaver's shuttle or distaff. Long misinterpreted, as I said, because most examples of the Sunday Christ bear no texts to explain them, these strange images are mostly silent, their message at first hidden. In some images drops or streams of blood connect each item to the suffering body. In another, above and to the side of the image, Saint Peter is depicted, his left arm raised to accept—or perhaps, reject—two souls at the gates of heaven.[2]

However, a few images do come with words that help us decipher their meaning. A Sunday Christ from Florence, for instance, bears the inscription: "Whomsoever does not keep Sunday holy and does not have devotion to Christ, God will condemn to eternal damnation." Another image from northern Italy bears an even more frightening warning: "By means of snares, the devils have caught those who have not yet honored and sanctified Sundays and the ordained feast days, and [made] it seem sweet to sin, in order to take us to bitter punishment."[3] These words make the meaning clear: the Sunday Christ is a Sabbatarian image. It's about what one should and should not do on the Lord's Day, how what one chooses to do on a Sunday affects both Christ and the believer for better or worse. To engage in trade, to engage in certain entertainments—so the image warns—*wounds* Christ. It also puts one's own soul in danger; it wounds believers too.

No idle warning, no myth, the Sunday Christ bore a truth more readily believed then than now. Medieval memory and history, you see, were different. The medieval mind erased distinctions of past and present in a manner we can hardly fathom now; ritual and art collapsed and conflated epochs within the premodern mind with a lack of historical consciousness we today find incredible. And that's because, as Jacques Maritain said of the medieval sense of self, the medieval soul "forgot itself for God." For the medieval person, before humanism's exaltation of the self, there was an "absence of the deliberately reflexive glance of the creature

---

2. Reiss, *Sunday Christ*, 11.
3. Reiss, *Sunday Christ*, 23.

on itself."[4] That is, the medieval person didn't think about herself as much as her modern descendants do, nor did she plot herself on a historical timeline as readily as we do today. And this, for her, brought past ages alive in a way we can't recreate for ourselves. It wasn't a stretch—either artistically, mnemonically, or theologically—for believers in the Middle Ages to think of an event from even the distant past as something really close to the present, as something even within the present.[5] It wasn't a stretch to believe what the Sunday Christ seemed to suggest, that the tools of one's trade and the toys of one's entertainment could indeed wound Christ alongside the other instruments of his passion. Because for medieval believers, Christ was indeed that close. By his incarnation, Christ was present not only on the altar but everywhere. Thus, it was wise to worry about what one did day in and day out, for it certainly mattered. Because what one did or did not do indeed touched Christ. Less the distance of history, more the closeness of memory, Christ was a vivid contemporary of medieval believers. Their art told the truth.

Today, however, our art is different. Our theological imagination is different. The truth the Sunday Christ told, its spiritual warning, is in our age harder to accept. Yet its essential truth remains. Perhaps we know better that we cannot wound Christ. Yet, what we do in our daily lives does affect our relationship with him. That is, what we do—even, and more than we realize, those things we think insignificant, morally neutral, harmlessly ordinary, just part of the job, what everyone else is doing, the plain, unthought sociological facts of our lives (what Jacques Ellul called our "style of life")—can indeed wound our union with Christ, even mortally, eternally.[6] The bloodied image perhaps is a metaphor; the way we see the world, so disenchanted today, means that we can only interpret the image, not see it as real but only as some strange primitive art to be deciphered. However, that we imagine this truth differently matters little, for the spiritual danger is the

---

4. Maritain, *Integral Humanism*, 157–61.
5. Le Goff, *History and Memory*, 7–13.
6. Ellul, *Presence of the Kingdom*, 121.

same, the end the same—the soul's loss of Christ. The stakes are the same. The warning stands.

Remember, though, we're talking about Sunday, the weekend, about what Christians do or don't do, about keeping or not keeping the Lord's Day. The Church is clear. Sunday is still just as holy, just as important as it ever was. Gathering for the Eucharist on Sunday is the "foundation and confirmation of all Christian practice." It's "at the heart of the Church's life." As Catholics, we're obligated to participate in the Sunday Eucharist. "Those who deliberately fail in this obligation commit a grave sin."[7] The Church obviously is still serious about Sunday. Our art may no longer offer such warnings, but the language of *obligation* and of *grave sin* suggests the Church still believes the Lord's Day necessary to Christian life, that without it the soul risks itself. Though the messaging may be more reserved, the message itself isn't.

But today how does one get this message across? How does one teach it, preach it? In the days of the Sunday Christ, keeping the Lord's Day was something enforced; not keeping it was punished. Missing Mass on Sunday, one could be fined or flogged or even be made to lead the procession barefooted the next Sunday Mass.[8] The consequences were public. And that's because Christians were expected to be visibly different. Saint Augustine in his day repeatedly reminded his congregation that they were different, that since they belonged to the City of God and not the earthly city, their actions should reflect their better destiny. Each New Year he railed against the customs and games of pagans. "They run to the theater: you go to church!" he thundered. "I am now speaking to true Christians: if your faith is different from that of others, if your hope is different, if your love is different, then lead different lives and show by your different conduct that your faith, hope, and charity are really different."[9] Being different was assumed; acting differently was expected. Saint John Chrysostom was perhaps fiercest of all. Hearing believers cheering at the horse races nearby,

---

7. *Catechism of the Catholic Church*, 2181, 2177.
8. Reiss, *Sunday Christ*, 54.
9. Augustine, *Sermons for Christmas and Epiphany* 17.2–3.

he hung his head in shame. "Is this bearable? Is this to be tolerated?" he began his fiery sermon afterward. For leaving the church and the spiritual sacrifice for worldly entertainments, Chrysostom accused his congregation of being taken captive by the devil. Those who chose the games or the theater over the church, he excommunicated: "This is why I'm telling you in advance and shouting loudly that if anyone deserts to the lawless corruption of the theatres after this exhortation and teaching, I won't receive him within these precincts, I won't administer the mysteries to him, I won't permit him to touch the holy table." Chrysostom explained himself saying he was simply being a good shepherd separating "the mangy sheep from the healthy ones so as not to give disease to the rest." He likened it to keeping a leper away from the rest of the community; "let's give them the chop," he said. He feared such irreligion was contagious, so he needed to counter it with "a teaching that's hotter than fire."[10] That's how he confronted the problem.

But I don't think any of that would work today. I'm not really sure it worked then. Berating people, policing them, I've learned, as a pastor, doesn't help. What does, though? The stakes, as I said, are the same. Keeping Sunday holy, honoring the Sabbath, making the weekend a time for human flourishing instead of exhaustion: all of it still matters; none of it should be jettisoned for some supposedly better way. Yet, how do we recover this lost human and sacred wisdom? How do we rediscover the path our ancestors took? How can we believe again it's the right path to follow? And how do we convince people any of this matters today?

To be honest, we probably can't. At least, we likely can't convince people on whatever scale we thought possible in the past—not without some new Pentecost, some awakening. Gone are the days of enforced faith, policed devotion—and for the better. Today we must offer this wisdom more gently, not by force, content to invite people to take up the challenge of this better, more human, more holy way of living. People must see and then seek this better life, not be shamed into it. The language of obligation, of grave sin,

---

10. Chrysostom, *Against the Games and Theatres*, PG 56.263–264, 268–269, in Allen and Mayer, *John Chrysostom*, 118–25.

Why Sunday Matters

the rhetoric of rules is honest about what's at stake; like a mother's stern warning, there's truth in it. But as Pope Saint John Paul II made clear, the language of obligation emerged only gradually; because of the "half-heartedness or negligence of some... the church had to make explicit the duty to attend Sunday Mass."[11] There is a better way than berating people to go to Mass on Sunday. For most people today, the on-ramp must be different. Perhaps, as Pope Saint John Paul II suggests, it's a matter of rediscovery. Perhaps the invitation must be more like what Jesus said to Andrew and the other disciple—"Come, and you will see" (John 1:39). Or maybe it must be more like what Jesus said to the rich young man—"If you wish..." (Matt 19:21). The invitation must stand alone—no nudging, no pressure, no behavioral manipulation. And so, we must admit that some, perhaps many at times, will not accept this invitation, that they won't want this more human, holier life, that, like the rich young man, some will walk away sad (Matt 19:22).

We must be content simply to share the wisdom which has always been there, never hidden but by our own noise. It's the wisdom God gave the Hebrews, first in the desert, in the Sinai Peninsula, when he commanded the people to gather manna each day but the seventh day, doubling what they collected on the sixth day so there would be enough to eat on the next. But why weren't the Hebrews permitted to gather manna on the seventh day? Because, as Moses told them, the seventh day "is a day of complete rest, the sabbath, sacred to the Lord" (Exod 16:23). Seemingly arbitrary, it's a curious thing to command in the middle of the desert. What was God doing? It seems he was folding his wandering, displaced people into the deepest reasons of things, into the most primeval and playful form of creation, into something far more enduring than their pilgrimage suggested (Prov 8:30–31). He was gathering them into the rhythm of creation itself. "God blessed the seventh day and made it holy, because on it he rested from all the work he had done in creation" (Gen 2:3). The seventh day is the first thing God ever called holy. It's the day he created rest—*menuha*. Rest, in this biblical sense, as Abraham Joshua Heschel put it, "is not a

---

11. John Paul II, *Dies Domini*, 47.

negative concept but something real and intrinsically positive." It's not simply non-activity but the gift of tranquility, peace, serenity. The Lord, like a shepherd, leads his people beside *menuhot* waters (Ps 23:2). "In later times," Heschel writes, "*menuha* became a synonym for life in the world to come, for eternal life."[12] That's what God offered his people wandering in the desert, to a people uprooted, displaced, homeless—eternity-like rest.

The Sabbath serves as a sign of the covenant between God and Israel (Exod 31:13). This is the origin of the religion of the Sabbath. Israel is commanded to remember to keep holy the Sabbath (Exod 20:8). When Moses calls the Sabbath a sign or token of the covenant, it comes after a lengthy description of the Tent of Meeting, how it's to be constructed and adorned. Sabbath and sanctuary belong together. "Keep my sabbaths, and reverence my sanctuary," God says (Lev 19:30; 26:2). The tabernacle, and then the temple, is the place where God draws near to his people and how eternity enters time. But as in the desert, God's desire to give his people *menuha*, his rest, remains. That's the purpose of the whole of religion, the law and its details—the gift of rest. But again, the question is whether one sees this or only rules. "It is for the law to clear the path; it is for the soul to sense the spirit," says Heschel.[13] The commandment is in essence only an invitation. The deeper question is whether one wants this rest of God.

It's rest which, when received, can't help but become liberation. The gift was offered to liberated people. The Decalogue begins by recalling Israel's liberation from Egypt: "I, the Lord, am your God, who brought you out of Egypt, that place of slavery" (Exod 20:2). Deuteronomy's rendering of the Decalogue ties the observance of the Sabbath to memory of Israel's enslavement in Egypt and to the Exodus. As Israel was liberated, so too should all things be liberated on the Sabbath—cattle, foreigners, servants and slaves. "For remember that you too were once slaves in Egypt, and the Lord, your God, brought you from there with his strong hand and outstretched arm. That is why the Lord, your God, has

---

12. Heschel, *Sabbath*, 22–23.
13. Heschel, *Sabbath*, 17.

commanded you to observe the sabbath day" (Deut 5:15). Among God's people such rest was a time of liberation not just weekly but also generationally. The sabbatical year and the jubilee year—every seventh and fiftieth year—were meant to bring rest to the land, equal provision for all; and, at least every half-century, it was meant to bring "liberty in the land for all its inhabitants" (Lev 25:1-22). Later in the prophets this Sabbath liberation becomes a call for justice. Only a fast that eliminates oppression and feeds the hungry is a genuinely delightful Sabbath, Isaiah suggested (Isa 58). Upon Judah, Jeremiah prophesied the sword and exile because they neglected Sabbath liberation. "You did not obey me by proclaiming your neighbors and kinsmen free," God spoke through the prophet (Jer 34:17). Injustice "desecrated my sabbaths," God said through Ezekiel (Ezek 20). Here too the logic was the same; here too the stakes were high. God offered his people rest, and in turn, God's people were to offer this rest to others. Such is the biblical origin of justice, its neglect the measure of injustice.

For Christians, though, what does this mean? How the earliest Christians kept the Sabbath and how their Eucharistic gatherings on the "Lord's day" (Rev 1:10) or the "first day of the week" (Acts 20:7; 1 Cor 16:2) developed into what we now call Sunday is its own unique and long-debated story.[14] In some places the Sabbath became a time for studying the Scripture while Sunday was less a time to rest and more a time for worship. In the fourth century when Constantine forbade work for everyone but farmers, for instance, he did so not that people would have time for rest but that they would be free to worship.[15] So how does the religion of Sabbath rest and liberation relate to followers of Jesus? The short answer is that God's Sabbath is given to us in Jesus Christ. "Now the promises were made to Abraham and his descendant," Paul wrote (Gal 3:16). The descendant of Abraham is Christ, in whom all believers live. Thus, the *menuha* God created on the seventh

---

14. Bradshaw and Johnson, *Origins of Feasts, Fasts, and Seasons in Early Christianity*, 3-28.

15. Bradshaw and Johnson, *Origins of Feasts, Fasts, and Seasons in Early Christianity*, 25.

day, which he gives his chosen people, he also gives to the Church in Christ. In this way—in Christ—the gift of the Sabbath is meant for Christians too. Christians often use these two terms interchangeably, but the Sabbath day and Sunday, from the perspective of religious history and practice, are distinct; one is not the other. The Sabbath, with its rest, points prophetically to the risen Christ, who *is* rest, whom we encounter on Sunday. In Christ, Sabbath rest is also given to the followers of Jesus. On Sunday, when Christians gather to celebrate the Eucharist, entering the Temple that is Christ, they too receive God's promised rest. The way Saint Augustine put it, belonging in Christ to the City of God, Christians will ultimately "become that seventh day," an endless Sabbath that dawns upon an eighth day, the Lord's Day, "which is to last forever," where the faithful shall be "at leisure for eternity," and where "we shall be still and see," and where "we shall love and we shall praise," seeing God who is all in all.[16] That's what believers experience in Christ: sacramentally and partially while still on pilgrimage, perfectly in blessedness. This is what the Church means saying, "Sunday fulfills the spiritual truth of the Jewish sabbath and announces man's eternal rest in God."[17] Christians are meant to have this rest too. What God gives the Jews he offers believers in Christ. So again, the stakes are the same; the promise and the warnings are the same. Understanding, as the fathers did, that between the Sabbath and the Lord's Day there are indeed differences due to time and the practices of each, nonetheless, the embodied wisdom of the Sabbath remains relevant for Christians. As Pope Saint John Paul II said, "the underlying reasons for keeping the Lord's Day holy—inscribed solemnly in the Ten Commandments—remain valid."[18] God's command to rest remains a command.

    It matters, then, that Christians tend not only to the "moral commandment inscribed by nature in the human heart" to worship God but also to the "rhythm of work and rest" given by God

---

16. Augustine, *City of God* 22.30.
17. *Catechism of the Catholic Church*, 2175.
18. John Paul II, *Dies Domini*, 62.

Why Sunday Matters

on the seventh day.[19] "What *we are* depends on what *the Sabbath is* to us," Heschel wrote.[20] This is true for Christians too. The Sabbath matters. Receiving and honoring God's rest is as important to the followers of Jesus as it was to God's people in the desert. It's existential, belonging to the question of what we are, who we are. Lost to this wisdom, to Sabbath rest and liberation, as Christians, as humans, we are impoverished and reduced, now neither as Christian or human as we should be. So why have we abandoned this wisdom, forgotten it almost entirely? How did we forget the Sunday Christ?

That is a unique and debated story. The tedious fact of human waywardness, of course, is first to blame. Even in the desert, it seems, the hearts of God's people went astray. "They shall never enter my rest," God swore in his anger once (Ps 95:11). Our waywardness today, though, seems also a by-product of modernity, the dividend of the practical ordering of contemporary life, the result of economic evolution. The Anglican theologian the late John Hughes called it the "Spirit of Utility," a conspiracy of factors that slowly changed everything. For Hughes it is "a rational, calculating, quantifying spirit, which seemed determinedly destructive of traditional modes of thought and life, with materialistic, anti-theological prejudices, levelling qualitative differences to one commensurable, measurable scale, bracketing out moral and theological concerns in order to occupy a purportedly 'neutral,' empirically desirable realm."[21] The medieval historian Jacques Le Goff spoke of the rise of this logic of utility in terms of a conflict between the "Church's time" and the "merchant's time." Le Goff thought it one of the major turnings in the mental history of the Middle Ages.[22] Ecclesiastical time liturgically ordered the imagination and practical life around the biblical facts of God's creation, his incarnation, and Christ's return. The Church's time—with its bells calling the faithful to prayer and Mass, announcing death and

---

19. *Catechism of the Catholic Church*, 2176, 2184.
20. Heschel, *Sabbath*, 89.
21. Hughes, *End of Work*, 217.
22. Le Goff, *Time, Work, and Culture in the Middle Ages*, 30.

burial—located life within its story. The merchant's time, however, was different. With its orderly bells marking the beginning and end of the workday, with the invention of the mechanical clock, merchant's time introduced organization, predictability, measurement—but for the mundane ends of commerce. As Lewis Mumford put it, once meant solely for prayer and sacred order, eventually "time-keeping passed into time-serving and time-accounting and time-rationing."[23] Punching in and out of work became as important and as measured as prayer. But conflict came when the bells of work and the bells of the Church failed to harmonize. As Le Goff put it, "If he remained Christian, he could not avoid rude confrontations and contradictions between time as he used it in his business and time in his religion without paying the price of mental conflict and practical trickery."[24] Business and religion were placed more and more at odds; and business increasingly won out. In 1536, for instance, Henry VIII abolished the *festa ferianda*; these were locally or nationally celebrated feast days which involved either partial or total abstention from work. They were abolished because they hindered productivity, impoverishing the people, so it was claimed.[25] This was just the beginning, the birth of the form of life which is ours today—life timed by the hours of our jobs, the quarters of profits, shopping seasons, retirement planning. Add to this, as supply to demand or as a dog to Pavlov's bell, the rise of consumer culture, ubiquitous advertising, those "strategies of desire" relentlessly luring us to want more, to purchase more.[26] Add also, as an addict forsakes everything for the high, all those de-skilling technologies, our screens dulling those more human habits of conversation and listening, empathy, and contemplation. It's not difficult to recognize the story of our contemporary waywardness, not hard to see how we got here.

23. Mumford, *Technics and Civilization*, 14.
24. Le Goff, *Time, Work, and Culture in the Middle Ages*, 41.
25. Duffy, *Stripping of the Altars*, 42.
26. Dichter, *Strategy of Desire*.

Why Sunday Matters

That is, to our present restlessness. There are many ways to describe it. Marx, following Hegel, talked about alienation.[27] Durkheim spoke of anomie. The former (and Maritain called it "the great flash of truth running through his work"[28]) names that felt divorce of self from nature, felt acutely under the conditions of modern labor when one's work is no longer one's own, when one is no longer a maker of anything but merely a cog in a machine, a body on a production line. The latter is that modern and almost always urban sense of derangement, the feeling of being caught between the pressures of work and home, between the pressures of social conformity and one's own sense of self.[29] Gabriel Marcel talked about *inquiétude*, that existential feeling of constriction, the anxiety we feel when who we are has been reduced to what we do, reduced entirely to our work, to what we can produce or consume.[30] The pressure we feel to keep pace with some external standard of achievement—some standard of education, some job, a certain income, to become a conspicuous consumer—is that restlessness we all at times feel. It's the unholy origin of the rat race. An almost collective compulsion, it is what both drives us and sometimes deranges us. More than overworking us, it ruins whatever rest or leisure or play we might seek. For instance, even if we are fortunate enough to afford leisure, vacations become merely periods of recuperation, a time for recharging the batteries, a time of rest for the sake of returning to work refreshed. Vacations serve work in our rat race world. Children's play becomes activity, and parents feel guilty wondering if their children are active enough. Every day must be scheduled; there must be no offseason. Play must be good for development; there must be some productive end to child's play. Again, if you can afford it, for the rat race begins early—in the nursery, sometimes as early as the baby shower—and it gets costly quickly. Because there's no time to waste and no expense worth sparing.

27. Berlin, *Karl Marx*, 113; Hughes, *End of Work*, 67.
28. Maritain, *Integral Humanism*, 181.
29. Durkheim, *Division of Labor in Society*, 291–308.
30. Keen, "Development of the Idea of Being," 107.

The Sunday Christ

And the result of this modern restlessness is sub-humanity. That's what Josef Pieper argued in *Leisure: The Basis of Culture*. Writing among the ruins of the Second World War, as everyone was focused on rebuilding nations and economies, Pieper feared that in the furor of reconstruction man had forgotten something important: leisure. "Now of all times, in the post-war years is not the time to talk about leisure," ran the objection.[31] But true leisure is essential, Pieper insisted, for without it, we wouldn't be human anymore.[32] He was talking about leisure in the ancient sense—as *skole*.[33] Pieper called it a mental and spiritual attitude whereby the intellect is freed for contemplation and the mind is liberated for understanding.[34] Humans are most human when they are at leisure, in contemplation. Pieper thought here in terms of Aristotelian and Christian contemplation, which he identified with Sabbath rest.[35] An aristocratic point that for some is not without problematic implications, it is nonetheless a point that should not be lost.[36] We suffer from the loss of genuine leisure a profound wound. The effects are not easy to see nor are they often dramatic, but they nonetheless cut deep. The prophecies of Huxley and Orwell have both come true. We suffer from a hollowness that we relentlessly struggle to fill with endless activity, endless consumption, and all with glistening sentimentality. But it never works. Seeking more and more, we're left with less and less. Sub-human beggars of a Nietzschean apocalypse, we've been robbed so completely of the treasures of our nature that now we are servants of screens, told whom to love and to hate, what to buy and even when to die. As Heschel put it, "our victories have come to resemble defeats. In spite of our triumphs, we have fallen victims to the work of our

---

31. Pieper, *Leisure*, 19.
32. Pieper, *Leisure*, 44.
33. Pieper, *Leisure*, 20.
34. Pieper, *Leisure*, 26–27, 40.
35. Pieper, *In Tune with the World*, 46.
36. Hughes, *End of Work*, 170.

hands; it is as if the forces we had conquered have conquered us."[37] All because we have forgotten the *menuha* God offers.

Hence the urgent need to rediscover God's given rest. But how? Were we to paint the Sunday Christ anew on the walls of churches today, a bloodied Jesus might be surrounded by a smartphone, a laptop, a football, a crosse or a hockey stick. However, I doubt such art would do anything but offend. How then might we meditate upon the Sunday Christ today? The invitation must be different, more humble, gentler. Certainly, our spiritual imagination is not that of our ancestors, but we must be no less truthful, no less convicted about what's at stake. We must be honest about spiritual wounds. Candid about our distractions and obstacles, our bad priorities, our idols, we must indeed lead with beauty, with the truth about how beautiful God's rest is, this rest created for us and for which we were created. But we must still be honest about our wounds. We must seek the goodness of God's rest more than fear what will become of us without it, yet at the same time we must see that our relationship with Jesus Christ can be wounded by what we have done and left undone. We can't be pushed. We must desire it. But still, we must meditate upon our wounds and the wounds of Christ, which is what the remainder of this book is about. Meditating on just a few of our everyday spiritual wounds, wounds we may not even recognize or are afraid to admit, we may at least begin to tend them, to dress them. For only then might we hide them within the wounds of Christ, in which is healing, and from which come the restful waters of a more genuine humanity—healing found only in the Sunday Christ.

---

37. Heschel, *Sabbath*, 27.

2

The Religion of Sports

Playing sports has become very important today . . .
—Pope Saint John Paul II

"Man, that sounds nice," he said. I was talking about nothing, how my kids did nothing. Talking to another dad around a campfire in Oklahoma as a pack of third-grade girls loudly roamed through the woods scaring bears as far away as Arkansas, it was an instance of honesty, staring at the fire. A moment of truth, it was a confession of exhaustion, each admitting to the other how he really felt.

Talking about what our kids did—the sports they were in, the teams they were on, all the games they played—I told him about our family's annual offseason, how during the winter our kids get bored, fight over the remote, and spend sometimes entire Saturdays doing nothing at all. You'd think my kid had been accepted to Notre Dame or Harvard the way I bragged about it. That's what sounded nice, this fellow dad admitted with a laugh, a little resignation too—doing nothing.

Why Sunday Matters

Not that there is any virtue in what we are doing, or rather, not doing. For us, family offseason is accidental. Our oldest kid tried basketball but didn't like it. No one in our family ever had hoop dreams. None are destined for the NBA much less a middle school roster. Also, dragging a Catholic-sized family (with the added anomaly of me being a priest) through one crowded gym and then another quickly became for my wife (who most weekends had to lead these expeditions alone) an exhausting chore. Better rather to declare an offseason and cut our losses, maybe take a karate lesson or two, go on a playdate, or visit grandparents. That became our "doing nothing"—doing something other than going from one game to another and then two more games after that. That's what I was bragging about, what sounded nice.

Again, there is no virtue in our family offseason. As I said, it's mostly an accident. And it is fading fast anyway as my oldest daughter plays softball now, and her younger sister is beginning to take up volleyball. They love softball and volleyball, and I love that they love those sports. But their teams play well into December and practice year-round. I don't remember that about the sports I played growing up, but what can you do? Our family offseason is fading away. The social pressure, imagined or real, is just too great. Good while it lasted, all that doing nothing, it sounded nice. It was nice. It was good.

But why does a family offseason sound nice? Why was it good while it lasted? Because we parents are exhausted. Quietly to one another we may admit that we're tired and worried about the rush of it all, but the social pressure to appear on top of our parenting game, doing what's best for our kids, silences most of us. Yet families are exhausted, one sees it on the faces of parents and children hurrying from one game and practice to the next. Standing on the sidelines one morning at a soccer game for my then-kindergartner, the contest barely half over, the dad next to me suddenly pulled his daughter out the game. "Get your things, darling. We've got to run," he said sweetly. He told the coach before the game they had to leave early. "She's got another game in thirty minutes," he said to me as he began to jog off the field. His daughter was on two other soccer teams and had two other games that day—a kindergartner. I saw that same devoted father later that day. He was tired; they were all very tired, he told me. It was all a rush, he admitted—weekend after weekend, each weekend the same. And he couldn't really make sense of it or explain it. He couldn't say if it was right or wrong, good or bad. That's just what their Saturdays and Sundays looked like. That was all there was to it.

But family weekends used not to be this way. There is a reason families are exhausted and kids are burning out. Because the demands youth sports put on families today is not normal. Youth sports have changed in recent decades and not for the better. "We all know that there are major problems in youth sports today," write Brenda Bredemeier and David Shields, two professors at the University of Missouri–St. Louis focused on education and character development.[1] David King, former athletic director at Eastern Mennonite University, describes the change he has witnessed in youth sports over his thirty-five-year career. "I've seen the landscape change dramatically," he says, change marked by overwork and fear. He writes,

> I've become increasingly concerned about the toll that current youth sports culture is taking on children, young people, and families. Families' dollars and time are stretched and stressed. Children are suffering overuse injuries and burning out at younger and younger ages. They're being asked to perform beyond appropriate developmental stages. They're failing to develop some of the intrinsic values that adults *assume* sports will teach them. Parents are damaging their relationships with their kids and with each other. And far too often, as we struggle to navigate this new terrain, we're driven not by love but by fear.[2]

It's also what many other athletic directors, coaches, scouts, psychologists, and doctors say about the problems endemic in this newer, busier, business of youth sports. Competition has been

---

1. Shields and Bredemeier, "Reclaiming Competition in Youth Sports," 129.
2. King and Starbuck, *Overplayed*, 10.

corrupted, write Bredemeier and Shields. Today, they argue, youth sports often carry a "dangerous virus," having become "increasingly professionalized."[3] The Aspen Institute's Sports and Society Program, arguing that today's culture of youth sports "ought to be disrupted," puts it this way: "Today, adult-led competition dominates and tryout-based, multi-season travel teams form as early as age 6, siphoning players from and support for in-town recreation leagues that serve all kids. We emphasize performance over participation well before kids' bodies, minds, and interests mature."[4] Kids playing sports today are fewer. Kids in any sort of physical education class, kids getting anywhere near the recommended amount of physical activity, also are fewer.[5] And those who do play are often not served well. The negative outcomes are several: "elite" pay-to-play exclusion, the normalizing of single-sport specialization leading to an increased number of injuries due to year-round play. This is the brave new world of youth sports today.

And it's largely a socioeconomic phenomenon. American sports have always put class distinctions on display, but with youth sports they are even more pronounced.[6] Derek Thompson, for *The Atlantic*, writes that, "among richer families, youth sports participation is actually rising. Among the poorest, it's trending down." In 2017, for example, only 34 percent of kids from families earning less than $25,000 played a team sport at least a single day as opposed to 69 percent of kids from families earning over $100,000.[7] The Aspen Institute reports that the "actual financial costs involved in facilitating a youth sport career at the elite levels range from an average of a few thousand dollars per year, to more than $20,000 per year in some sports." Unsurprisingly, the report

---

3. Shields and Bredemeier, "Reclaiming Competition in Youth Sports," 113, 129.

4. Aspen Institute Sports and Society Program, "Sport for All, Play for Life: A Playbook to Get Every Kid in the Game."

5. Aspen Institute Sports and Society Program, "Sport for All, Play for Life: A Playbook to Develop Every Student through Sports."

6. Overman, *Protestant Ethic and the Spirit of American Sport*, 152.

7. Thompson, "American Meritocracy Is Killing Youth Sports."

continues, "participation in organized sports is not feasible for a majority of kids growing up in lower income families."[8] "This isn't a story about American childhood; it's about American inequality," Thompson writes. "Youth sports has become a pay-to-play machine."[9] And the overall negative effect is that "we ignore, push aside, and fail to develop the human [and athletic] potential of most children."[10]

But even kids fortunate enough to play are often playing too much. And it's hurting them. As Fr. Patrick Kelly, who explores the intersection of theology, sports, and human development, writes, "Today young people who participate in sport suffer from overuse injuries at a dramatically increased rate compared to thirty years ago."[11] During the COVID pandemic, as elective surgeries were postponed to relieve overstressed healthcare systems, there was an uproar among many parents upset over delayed care their young athletes needed, while in turn many sports medicine clinics suffered financially. Because, although not critical (especially in light of a global pandemic), the demand for youth sports medicine today is tremendous; it's become big business. The primary factor driving demand is that more kids are specializing in one sport, playing the same sport too much, leading to overuse injuries. As Jon Solomon, from the Aspen Institute, writes, "as the trend toward early specialization in sports has grown, so has the need for medical care. Among children 14 and under, more than 3.5 million receive medical treatment for sports injuries annually."[12] Repeated surveys show that injuries are now top of mind for parents, concussions foremost.[13] For instance, a decade ago, when writers for ESPN and

8. Aspen Institute Sports and Society Program, "Research Brief."
9. Thompson, "American Meritocracy Is Killing Youth Sports."
10. Aspen Institute Sports and Society Program, "Sport for All, Play for Life: A Playbook to Get Every Kid in the Game."
11. Kelly, "Youth Sport and Spirituality," 136.
12. Solomon, "Injury Treatments Are Suspended Due to Public Health Needs."
13. Aspen Institute Sports and Society Program, "Youth Sports Facts: Challenges."

The Atlantic asked Pop Warner's medical director to explain why fewer kids were playing football, he answered that fear of brain injuries were "the No. 1 cause."[14] It's a fear not entirely without merit given what we have learned about brain injuries: that as kids grow, get bigger and faster, so too does risk of concussion, and not just for kids playing football but even for those engaged in sports like wrestling and cheerleading.[15]

But aside from social consequences and bodily harm, issues of inequality and injury, which are all part of the brave new world of youth sports, there are also damaging spiritual effects. Worrying about the possible spiritual dangers of youth sports goes back a long way. Some of the fathers of the Second Vatican Council raised such concerns. They feared sports could tempt too many people away from the practice of religion.[16] It was not an unfounded fear. As the authors of *On the Eighth Day: A Catholic Theology of Sport* write, one could argue that "sport has gradually displaced traditional religion on a functional level." They continue, "Today, many spend their Sundays with sport rather than in church. Sport gives people the type of social connections, traditions, identity, and even meaning that is usually found in religion. To put it simply, the pews are empty, but the bleachers are full."[17] Sports have been compared to religion for years.[18] Scholars have long debated whether sports should be thought of as a religion. Joseph Price, for instance, argues that for millions of Americans "sports constitute a popular form of religion by shaping their own world and sustaining their ways of engaging it. Indeed, for many, sports are elevated to a kind of divine status, in what I would call an American apotheosis."[19] Others, however, disagree; but the question is academic.[20]

14. "Can Youth Football Be Saved? (And Should It Be?)"
15. "Can Youth Football Be Saved? (And Should It Be?)"
16. Hoven et al., *On the Eighth Day*, 8.
17. Hoven et al., *On the Eighth Day*, 6.
18. Alpert, *Religion and Sports*, 11.
19. Price, *From Season to Season*, 216.
20. Higgs and Braswell, *Unholy Alliance*.

The Religion of Sports

What isn't academic, however, is that in their likeness to religion, sports often seem to offer falsely what only authentic religion truly offers, and that is the genuine experience of transcendence. In that sense, sports today, and youth sports especially, is functionally another religion proclaiming, as Saint Paul would put it, "a different gospel" (Gal 1:6). As theologian Stephan Goertz argues, the problem is that sports offer "a type of transcendence that lacks a distinct transcendental reference point."[21] Or, as longtime sports chaplain Bernhard Maier put it, sports, although meaningful in significant ways, also "can distract us from more elevated things."[22] That is, if we judge sports to be a religion, then it's a bad religion, shallow at best. For all that sports can offer is limited or counterfeit transcendence, something that either doesn't last or is false. This is why, for instance, John Thompson, legendary former Georgetown basketball coach, kept on display in his office a deflated basketball, to remind his players not to pin everything—their sense of personal value, their understanding of meaning—on a game they will one day stop playing.[23] For basketball, like any sport, is not equipped to provide truly enduring meaning and value. Those things are more reliably and lastingly found in family, relationships, community, and religion. Which is why the religious rhetoric of sports is ultimately problematic, because at a certain point some may think that it's more than a metaphor. An ESPN ad for college football, for instance, calling it the "Greatest Story Ever Played," is clearly just clever or silly advertising, undoubtedly harmless. But what about when Tom Brady and Michael Strahan helped found The Religion of Sports, a media company selling the idea that "to feel the power of sport—and to truly believe—is to experience religion"?[24] What happens when we earnestly pretend that sports is a religion, or earnestly treat it like a religion, putting sports in people's lives in place of it? The answer is that the religion of sports eventually

21. Goertz, "Sport as a Sign of the Times," 199.
22. Maier, "Sport as a Pastoral Opportunity," 219.
23. Hoven et al., *On the Eighth Day*, 133.
24. https://www.religionofsports.com/. Also, Hoven et al., *On the Eighth Day*, 56.

Why Sunday Matters

falls flat. The promised transcendence perceived and desired in superstars like Tom Brady turns out to be merely advertising, a peddled idolatry meant only to form consumers instead of believers and saints. Eventually the emptiness of the religion of sports is revealed, that all of it is destined to fade along with all the other fleeting glories of the world rather than endure as a world without end. One is eventually left with nothing.

Christians should find it troubling that treating sports like religion leads to nothing. It's reminiscent of Screwtape's words to Wormwood: "To get the man's soul and give him *nothing* in return—that is what really gladdens our Father's heart."[25] It's a demonic goal to leave a person with nothing, entirely and eternally empty. But always it's a subtle exchange, barely noticeable—trading religion for sports. At first, it looks like time management and team commitment. But soon what is sacrificed are the habits and virtues necessary to the practice of genuine religion. For that's a significant part of what religion is; from *religare*, meaning "bind together," religion comprises those habits and practices which bind us to God.[26] The discipline of religion, to put it that way, manifest in routines and rhythms like regular Sunday worship, is replaced by practices, games, and tournaments. Instead of going to Mass on Sunday, a family goes to the game, more than likely several games. And thus, in short order and simple as that, sports functionally become a religion rivaling genuine religion, eventually replacing it, no matter how much one plies one's spirituality and random religious observance with sentimentality—or "lip service," Jesus called it (Matt 15:8). It's a harsh assessment. At first blush, it seems overblown to suggest that when sports functionally replace religion, religion dies. But that's exactly what high school coach Albert Zander sees. "Nothing is sacred anymore, and Sunday has become a tournament day," he says. "I have observed long enough to see that the kid grows up and has no faith of their own because the message was communicated to them through the family's actions

---

25. Lewis, *Screwtape Letters*, letter IX.
26. Aquinas, *Summa Theologiae* IIa IIae q. 81, a. 1.

that sports are more important than their church, faith, or God."[27] David King sees the same:

> Parents who have driven their children from tournament to tournament, weekend after weekend, year after year, become distraught when their child goes to college and leaves the faith behind. Yet for years the parents have been communicating to their child that their faith community, communal worship, and church aren't important. Parents rarely intend to communicate that, and following Christ might be very important to the parents themselves. Regardless, they have sent a clear message to their children that their faith community is not more important than their athletic schedule.

But it's not just about church attendance, missing Sunday Mass. As King continues, it's about "the cumulative effect and decisions about sports and church involvements that communicate to children what we value and what we hope they will value."[28] That matters because what we value is our relationship with Jesus Christ and the rest he gives to those who believe and live in him (Matt 11:28). Here we come to the heart of the matter: the fundamental spiritual danger posed by today's culture of youth sports. Here we touch the spiritual wound of youth sports. Scheduling the Church, worship, and the sacraments out of our lives, rendering them at best randomly sentimental things only occasionally experienced, replacing the discipline and rhythm of genuine religion with the discipline and rhythm of sports—no matter how much we protest—Jesus does inevitably get pushed out of our lives. And those moments we're meant to encounter Christ are replaced by moments only at best fleetingly transcendent. Youth sports lived this way Sunday by Sunday, with a commitment once given to the Christian community, does in fact wound one's relationship with Christ. To revisit the image of the Sunday Christ, as I suggested in the previous chapter, were it found on the walls of churches today, it would be surrounded by things like a football helmet or a soccer

---

27. King and Starbuck, *Overplayed*, 132–33.
28. King and Starbuck, *Overplayed*, 132–33.

ball. Because what we Christians are doing to ourselves, what we Christian parents are doing to our children, is indeed spiritually wounding. Giving as much of ourselves to youth sports as we do today reduces us, stealing from us the real and lasting rest only God gives, leaving us only hurried, rushed. From game to game and practice to practice, today's culture of youth sports often leaves children burned out or injured; but if not that, after the games have all been played, our kids are often left without the human and spiritual formation necessary to find meaning anywhere else, faithlessly empty in a brutal world. A different kind of nothing—unlike the nothing my kids do during our family offseason—this nothing is the death of faith, Christ lost to those who were just too busy.

So, how did we get here? How did youth sports become potentially so damaging, something even the Aspen Institute believes should be "disrupted"? We should first note what sociologists like Hilary Levey Friedman say about "social reproduction."[29] Inspired—or, intimidated—by books like Amy Chua's *Battle Hymn of the Tiger Mother*, parents, Friedman argues, act rationally by doing whatever they can to win for their children the credentials necessary to get into good schools, find success, achieve the good life, and "socially reproduce." For parents, it's often an all too powerful compulsion. No matter how ambivalent about the competitive ethos of activities like youth soccer or dance, the parents Friedman studied were still not willing to opt out. Whatever their reservations, "no one wanted to deny their child an opportunity to succeed. No one was willing to take the chance of not enrolling their kids in competitive activities, especially when all of their classmates appeared to be playing to win all the time."[30] This explains in part the overall busyness many American families experience, youth sports being a significant contributor. And that's because for a long time Americans have considered sports a social ladder.[31] Although clearly *not* a good investment—as King and Starbuck insist, "the odds show that youth sports is one of the

29. Friedman, *Playing to Win*, x.
30. Friedman, *Playing to Win*, xv.
31. Overman, *Protestant Ethic and the Spirit of American Sport*, 150.

worst 'investments' you'll ever make"—the drive to do whatever is thought necessary for our children's success creates an almost endless demand for "elite" travel teams, year-round play, and harmful specialization.[32] Such compulsion, generated often by fear, creates and sustains a youth sports industry designed more for profit than for child development or wellbeing. "These leagues make money. And they depend on recruiting kids—who are typically honored to be recruited—to make money," write King and Starbuck.[33] The pressure to chase whatever imagined good youth sports is supposed to provide results in what Richard Reeves calls "opportunity hoarding," the scramble to achieve whatever is deemed socially valuable.[34] Hence the race to join the most selective teams, play in the best tournaments, chase prestigious championships. And again, the race exacerbates existing socioeconomic disparities. As pay-to-play "elite" teams attract more kids whose parents are wealthy enough to pay, more kids whose parents can't afford it are left out, excluded from not just the benefits of play and team sports but from whatever are the imagined social benefits so many families are aiming to win. As Derek Thompson writes, "sports have come to resemble just another pre-professional program, with rising costs, hyper-specialization, and massive opportunity-hoarding among the privileged."[35] Such is the pressure we feel as parents, explaining our sense of inadequacy, our anxiety, our financial mismanagement, our sense of guilt that we're not doing enough, our worry we're wasting precious years of childhood driving to yet another forgettable game. Such is what so many parents feel but are afraid to admit because other parents seem to be doing just fine, at least on the surface.

Such is the lie. But again, how did it all start? What's the story behind the contemporary parental compulsions making youth sports so problematic? Following the medieval historian Philippe Ariès, it's a story born of the evolution of the modern family.

32. King and Starbuck, *Overplayed*, 190.
33. King and Starbuck, *Overplayed*, 81.
34. Reeves, *Dream Hoarders*.
35. Thompson, "American Meritocracy Is Killing Youth Sports."

Why Sunday Matters

Before the rise of the widespread education of children, Ariès argued, parents were far less sentimental about things like children and family. "The family was a moral and social, rather than a sentimental reality."[36] This changed, however, as families began to have fewer children and as more of them went away to school. In class all day children participated less and less in the adult world and, in a sense, created a separate world of childhood with its own realm and imaginary. Such is how childhood was "discovered," Ariès insisted.[37] Or, as Neil Postman put it, for a long time childhood was "invisible," certainly not conceived as its own distinct sociological category as it is today.[38]

But these newly "discovered" children couldn't be left to their own designs. They had to be educated. John Calvin was clear, children were "obnoxious" and had to be disciplined and trained.[39] Thus was born a "model of Protestant parenting" that, when met with "emerging scientific precepts of child development," would ultimately give us our modern moral intuition that childhood was something to be managed, an intuition that would only grow stronger as child labor decreased and compulsory education increased.[40] Thus, when the question of what to do with children after school found its answer in the rise of leisure and organized sports, the notion that the precious time of childhood was something to be disciplined and controlled would eventually transform our understanding of sports and play into something it had never been before—a kind of work.

But Christians, especially religious leaders, were at first wary of organized sports. "Before 1850 most Protestant groups condemned sports because sports diverted attention and consumed energy that could have been spent in the exercise of faith."[41] Only

36. Ariès, *Centuries of Childhood*, 368.
37. Ariès, *Centuries of Childhood*, 320.
38. Postman, *Disappearance of Childhood*, 18.
39. Overman, *Protestant Ethic and the Spirit of American Sport*, 242.
40. Overman, *Protestant Ethic and the Spirit of American Sport*, 245.
41. Price, "From Sabbath Proscriptions to Super Sunday Celebrations," in Price, *From Season to Season*, 17.

slowly, due to the influence of "muscular Christianity" in the latter half of the nineteenth century, did the leaders of Protestant Christianity come to approve of organized sports. Sports organized along secular lines, to be sure, continued apace, but with the rise of the YMCA, figures like Amos Alonzo Bragg and James Naismith in the nineteenth century and organized church leagues and groups like the Fellowship of Christian Athletes in the twentieth century, Christian churches came to embrace fully the world of modern sports. And Catholics soon followed. The American Catholic Youth Organization was founded as an alternative and rival to the Protestant YMCA, championed by people like Bishop Bernard J. Sheil who brought kids from vastly different backgrounds together to take up everything from checkers to boxing.[42]

But almost as soon as Christian leaders baptized organized sports, Hilary Levey Friedman argues, the game changed. The Progressive Era notion that athletics would prepare children to become fit laborers in industrial society gave rise to a whole range of athletic and competitive ventures from New York City's Public School Athletic League for Boys in 1903 to spelling bees, music, and memory competitions, and piano tournaments. All of it was meant to raise children up to be good citizens and workers. However, not everyone agreed that all this competition was good. "At the same time, many physical education professionals stopped supporting athletic competition for children because of worries that leagues supported competition for only the best athletes, leaving others behind."[43] Early in the twentieth century there was significant pushback against the rise of competitive sports and activities for young children. The concern was that such competition was harmful for young children. That's why "organized youth competition left the school system." That's why today, for instance, we don't have elementary school sports leagues. But that didn't put an end to it, for organized youth sports and other competitive

---

42. Hoven et al., *On the Eighth Day*, 152–55.

43. Friedman, *Playing to Win*, 27–29. See also, Friedman, "When Did Competitive Sports Take Over American Childhood?"

activities "did not leave American childhood."[44] In fact, competitive youth sports were only getting started. As schools left the game, organizations like Pop Warner Football, in 1929, and Little League Baseball, in 1939, got in the game. And, in the late 1970s, after the Amateur Athletic Union shifted its focus away from the Olympics to America's youth, competition in children's sports increased dramatically, giving rise to the professionalization of coaches, young athletes, and youth sports as a whole.[45] Also, add to this the notion youth sports offers kids an "admissions boost" when applying for college—something "far from guaranteed," Friedman says—and the demand for youth sports designed to give kids an advantage only grew.[46] Enter in this latter era of youth sports paid coaches, "elite" travel teams, kids specializing in one sport, and national championships for eight-year-olds.[47] And, of course, enter family exhaustion and childhood burnout.

This is the brave new world of youth sports. This is how we got here. From a confluence of several factors—an evolved sentimental appreciation of childhood, religious and scientific notions of parenting, pedagogical reserve and economic opportunism—the modern phenomenon of youth sports emerged. And it has made youth sports something unlike what it used to be, *play*. We've instead made it more like work. As Friedman puts it, "It is not a stretch to say that many young athletes and performers are now young professionals."[48] This is why so many parents feel pressure to push their kids into more activities and to sign them up to play on more teams. This is why parents are worn out and kids are burned out. From a dad who pulls his kindergartner early from a game because she's got two more games to play that day to some of the more absurd examples Friedman notes—like the father who gave over legal custody of his daughter to her figure skating coach

44. Friedman, "When Did Competitive Sports Take Over American Childhood?"
45. Friedman, *Playing to Win*, 30–31.
46. Friedman, *Playing to Win*, 13–14.
47. Friedman, *Playing to Win*, 34–36.
48. Friedman, *Playing to Win*, 33.

The Religion of Sports

to help her chase Olympic dreams—the world of youth sports today is not healthy.[49] Youth sports today as likely inhibits human flourishing as helps it. And we parents should just be honest about that, start talking to each other about it, and start doing things differently, doing better for our children.

"Yet our victories have come to resemble defeats." We recall again Abraham Joshua Heschel's words.[50] Here we are forced to contemplate again the rest we've lost, the *menuha* God offers. Heschel was talking about modern life as a whole, the ill effects of our industrial, commercial, and technological age. But it applies here too. What has become of youth sports belongs to that larger modern phenomenon, the rise of a rushed, unrestful world—a world without the Sabbath. From the standpoint of human flourishing and family wellbeing, youth sports have in many ways become parasitic, an obstacle to happiness. From a spiritual standpoint, youth sports often wound our relationship with Christ, scheduling us away from Christ and his Church, thereby stealing from us the rest and grace our souls need. In many ways youth sports have become enemies to humanity as well as to sanctity. They have become in many instances enemies of the Church. As Christians, we must no longer believe in the inherent goodness of youth sports; that is indeed a belief "dangerous to assume."[51] It's a myth, philosopher Daniel Dombrowski writes, that we should take "with a grain of salt." In his experience, "for every young athlete who is morally improved by participation in youth sports there is another athlete who may have been encouraged to become morally worse by athletic competition." "Youth sports *might* help your children and adolescents develop into responsible citizens and into admirable adults. But it might do the exact opposite too," he warns.[52] That youth sports are automatically good for your child should not be assumed, for there are indeed serious problems with youth sports today. But parents often feel alone in their ambivalence and

---

49. Friedman, *Playing to Win*, 35.
50. Heschel, *Sabbath*, 27.
51. Hoven et al., *On the Eighth Day*, 126.
52. Dombrowski, "What Is Sport? What Should It Be?," 22–23

concern. Yet they aren't alone. Which is why we must simply be more honest about this and start talking to one another.

But what should Christian parents do? What should the Church do? Youth sports is as prominent in the Catholic Church, in its schools and parochial leagues, as anywhere else. Catholics are deeply invested in youth sports. Yet, as Stephan Goertz asks, "Does the Church realize what's going on?"[53] In many ways, the answer is clearly no. Too many bishops, too many pastors, too many school administrators, and too many Catholic parents simply have not thought about it, have not been critical enough of the assumptions we make about the goodness of youth sports. As if it's a different world outside their immediate pastoral concern, few clergy think about youth sports at all. As if it poses no spiritual threat to the souls they are called to shepherd, too many clergy don't see the wolves. In fact, we clergy often help the wolves chase down the sheep, for they seem quite well-meaning wolves. This is certainly a dramatic way to put it, perhaps too dramatic, even insulting. But what if what we hold to be true about the practice of the faith and the necessity of Christ's rest is indeed true? What if gutting the practice of the faith for youth sports is indeed spiritually disastrous, spiritually deadly even? What then excuses our complacency? What justifies our conformity with the world?

How should Catholics and Catholic institutions think about youth sports today? What should they do? Are youth sports our Egypt, something we need only to escape? Or is the world of youth sports something Christians need not leave but instead work to redeem? But is that even possible? And if it is possible, what would that look like?

---

53. Goertz, "Sport as a Sign of the Times," 204.

3

Pure Play

> Holiness and play tend to overlap.
> —Johan Huizinga

The Romans went about it all wrong. If they wanted to wipe Christians off the face of the earth, they didn't need to arrest them or try them, persecute or kill them. They didn't need to jail them, crucify them, burn their bodies, use them as torches, or throw them into amphitheaters. That Saint Ignatius of Antioch should have ever needed to dream of pulling lions down on top of him, hoping their teeth would grind his flesh like wheat, wasn't necessary.[1] That Saint Perpetua and Saint Felicity should have been made a bloody spectacle, one gored and the other crushed, killed by cattle; or that the remains of dead Christians in France should have been dumped into the river, was misguided.[2] None of it needed to happen. If Tertullian was right, that "the blood of Christians is seed," that the death of the martyrs gives life to the Church, then,

---

1. Ignatius of Antioch, *To the Romans* 4.1, in Grant, *Apostolic Fathers*.
2. *Martyrdom of Saints Perpetua and Felicitas* 20; *Martyrs of Lyons* 1.62–63, in Musurillo, *Acts of the Christian Martyrs*.

as a program of religious extermination, persecuting Christians—making them a spectacle, murdering them—failed miserably.[3] It didn't work.

Better something else. Better to have made a spectacle for them than of them. Perhaps if the ancients weren't so bloodthirsty, they would have understood better the power of distraction over destruction. If only the Romans had started a few youth boxing leagues or organized a few trigon competitions; if only they had better vested these activities with the notion they naturally instilled virtue or secured coveted social rewards; if only they had left the Christians' belief in Jesus unchallenged; if only, instead of violently opposing Christianity, the Romans merely played their games gleefully alongside their severe, unwelcoming, sober Christian neighbors; if only, after saying a few nice things about their faith, they simply asked Christians to join in their games, perhaps on Sundays, would Christianity have survived a century? Or were the early Christians in fact tempted thus, only that their faith was strong enough to resist? I wonder. Would early Christianity have survived the cultural allure and power of today's youth sports? I'm not sure.

My assessment of the world of youth sports and other similar competitive activities, as they are widely experienced today, is harsh. Given especially that so many see nothing wrong, that I would warn of the spiritual dangers of these activities, speak of spiritual disaster, compare it to ancient Rome's persecution of Christians, I understand well that I may be easily dismissed or strongly opposed. There are, however, plenty of parents alert to these dangers, many as concerned as I am. To speak personally from my oddly intertwined vocation as both father and priest, what worries me most is the spiritual damage I see done to our overscheduled children as they are scheduled away from both the dinner table and the altar, from meaningful relationships with family members and friends and, most of all, from a meaningful relationship with Jesus Christ. What worries me are the wounds I see on the souls of so many children and parents, wounds of

---

3. Tertullian, *Apologeticus* 50.14.

Pure Play

an overachieving unhappiness, a spiritually dead but material flourishing.

But does that mean Christians shouldn't have anything to do with youth sports or that Christian parents should keep their kids from activities like dance and piano? Saint Jerome thought girls should never play the flute.[4] Should we follow suit? Should we revive old Puritan hatreds, declaring all of it immoral and irreligious? Not at all. On the contrary, Christians should continue to embrace these activities. In fact, *more* children should participate in sports. Part of the problem today, as we've seen, is that too few children play any sport at all. Christians should want to reverse that trend. The problem is not that Christians participate in youth sports and other activities, the problem is how.

Christians have long been involved in sports. One could argue that many of the sports we play and watch today wouldn't exist without Christianity, or at least not without the Christians who invented them. Basketball, for example, was a Christian sport, at least as the Presbyterian minister James Naismith first imagined it. However one interprets Paul's use of athletic imagery in the New Testament (it does not imply, for instance, that Paul was familiar with sports or approved of them) Christians have nonetheless positively engaged in sports for a very long time.[5] Even Chrysostom, who, as we have seen, railed against the games, nonetheless believed in the value of sports.[6] In the Middle Ages, when the church yard was the only common land available, villagers often played their games there. Worship, rest, and play were the natural elements of an ordinary Sunday. "After the sermon and the sacraments in the morning, villagers lounged or played on Sunday afternoon."[7] Games, athletics, even dancing have been part of Jesuit curricula since the seventeenth century.[8] Founder of the modern Olympics Pierre de Coubertin, himself a product of Jesuit

---

4. Jerome, *Select Letters*, 107.
5. Koch, "Biblical and Patristic Foundations for Sport," 86–87.
6. Kelly, "Christians and Sport," 40.
7. Baker, *Sports in the Western World*, 45.
8. Ariès, *Centuries of Childhood*, 88.

education, got the Olympics' motto—*citius, altius, fortius*—off his Dominican friend, a priest, Henri Didon. Belgian missionaries carried their love of soccer to Africa.[9] In Italy, in the first decades of the twentieth century, the Church encouraged Catholic youth sports as a way to fight secularism and fascism. Pope Pius XII considered youth sports vitally important to the Church's mission. The Church's care for the whole person, soul *and* body, as well as its concern for the perfection of virtue, meant that the Church was bound to care about the world of sports.[10] Examples of Christian engagement with sports abound. Sports are inseparable from the Christian experience, which is why to suggest that Christians should retreat from the world of sports is plainly contrary to the Christian spirit. It's a nonstarter.

So how then should Christians think about sports? Particularly, how should we think about *youth* sports? Pope Saint John Paul II said we should think about sports with an "attitude of redemption." *Giving the Best of Yourself*, the 2018 document summarizing the Church's understanding of sports as it relates to its mission, published by the Vatican's Dicastery for Laity, Family and Life, leads with just such an attitude of redemption. The Church must raise its voice "in the service of sport," because sport cannot interpret itself. What the Church offers is a "vision of sport that is grounded in a Christian understanding of the human person and just society." That is, the Church serves to remind Christians how sports fit within the larger game of life. When rooted in respect for human dignity and committed to justice and open to human destiny, sports serve what the Church has always prized, the "integral development" of each person.[11] Sports matter to the Church because sports matter to the whole person, the soul as well as the body. In the Church's mind, at least, Christian parents, Catholic educators, and clergy should be agents of redemption in the world of sports. But today that means, as Clark Power, the founder of Play Like a Champion, puts it, we Christians should "reclaim our

9. Hoven et al., *On the Eighth Day*, 24.
10. Lixey, "Sport in the Magisterium of Pius XII," 109.
11. Dicastery for Laity, Family and Life, *Giving the Best of Yourself* 1.1–2.1.

prophetic tradition" in the world of sports.[12] Again, because sport cannot interpret itself; because sports, in fact, often fall victim to other interpretations, "ideological or even amoral and inhuman."[13] Which is precisely the crisis. The fight is for the humanity and soul of sports for the sake of the souls and humanity of our children. That may sound dramatic; after all, we're talking about youth sports, games. But it does in fact matter as much as that. What's at stake isn't just a game.

We must realize that the redemption of sports begins with the redemption of play. Again as Hilary Levey Friedman said, pointing to the rigid hierarchies of youth sports, full-time paid coaches, and year-round seasons, too many young athletes today are "young professionals."[14] According to the Aspen Institute's Sports and Society Program, for generations, "casual play" was the "foundational experience" of America's children. "But the era of the sandlot or unstructured play, of making up games and playing with friends for hours on end, is largely gone." And so, says the Aspen Institute, we need to "reintroduce free play where possible." For them, this is a moral ought "given the science."[15]

It's science that also resonates with Christian thought, for when we begin to think about play theologically, we soon find ourselves thinking about the more primeval realities of our faith—things like contemplation, creation, and God. For play is woven into just these sacred things. Saint Thomas Aquinas, for instance, famously likened play to contemplation: one because, as the contemplation of wisdom is enjoyable so is play; and two, because play "has no purpose beyond itself."[16] This latter feature of *pure* play—its purposelessness—is what brings it so near the sacred, Saint Thomas thought, for it replicates the play of divine Wisdom. Saint Thomas

---

12. Power, "Playing Like a Champion Today," 97.

13. Dicastery for Laity, Family and Life, *Giving the Best of Yourself* 2.1.

14. Friedman, *Playing to Win*, 33.

15. Aspen Institute Sports and Society Program, "Sport for All, Play for Life: A Playbook to Get Every Kid in the Game," 7, 14.

16. Aquinas, "Prologue to the Commentary on Boethius' *De Hebdomadibus*," 527–28.

in this brief text points to Proverbs: "Then I was beside him as his craftsman, and I was his delight day by day, playing before him all the while" (Prov 8:30). The analogy Saint Thomas makes, using this text, is that as divine Wisdom seeks nothing else but to play eternally before God, contemplation seeks nothing else in just the same way, yearning as well only for Wisdom-like pleasure. Beyond this spiritual theology of contemplation, this passage also says something about the theology of creation. That playful Wisdom is also a "craftsman" suggests that creation (the universe, the world, you, me) is also in some sense play, that we are the created objects of God's play. To put it philosophically, creation is not necessary; it needn't have happened at all. Like a game, there is no purpose for which the world was made, no purpose beyond creation itself. God could just as well have not created anything, but instead he created the heavens and the earth and called it good, much like a child at play rejoices in his or her own unnecessary little world. But although unnecessary in this philosophical and playful sense, creation is still meaningful, again, as a game is meaningful with its world of rules and goals and ways to win and lose.

This idea is not original to Saint Thomas. The likeness of creation to play was noted in ancient pagan thought. Hugo Rahner in his classic work, *Man at Play*, highlights this. The Creator is the *Logos-child*, "the infant Logos who holds the sphere of the world within his playing hands."[17] Heraclitus likened the Creator to both king and child. "The Aeon is a child at play, playing draughts. The kingly rule is as a child's." This paradoxical image of power and playfulness exposes the "metaphysical nature of creation," Rahner says, that God in a way is "a playing God."[18] Human beings, therefore, are in a sense God's playthings; on this both the ancients and Church fathers agreed. We should consider ourselves "as a children's game played by God," said Saint Maximus the Confessor. Plato said the same.[19] But knowing that human beings are God's playthings doesn't denigrate us. Instead, it points to our likeness

17. Rahner, *Man at Play*, 23.
18. Rahner, *Man at Play*, 17–20.
19. Rahner, *Man at Play*, 17, 31.

Pure Play

to God, suggesting the reason why we humans instinctively do things like play and pray. Because we are created as play; we are created to play. God is *Deus ludens* and the human creature is *homo ludens*.[20] Human play, therefore, Rahner argues, "is an attempt to approximate the Creator." Plotinus said play strives for *theoria*—contemplation—just as Saint Thomas argued.[21] Play reveals something about our nature as well as our destiny, that its beginning and its perfection is rooted in a playful God. This in turn reveals the "sacral secret" of all play, that it is always in some measure a yearning for heaven, yearning for the eternal play of divine Wisdom, "for that superlative ease in which even the body, freed from its earthly burden, moves to the effortless measures of a heavenly dance."[22] That is, rest—*menuha*. Here we come again to the heart of the matter, to what is so dangerous about the loss of pure play—for culture, for souls.

At the end of *Homo Ludens*, his classic study of play and culture, Johan Huizinga observed that as Western civilization grew more complex, pure play began to disappear. "All Europe donned the boiler-suit" at the start of the Industrial Revolution, he wrote, and hasn't changed clothes since.[23] Play, slowly dislocated from its primeval place within culture, was eventually divorced from things like ritual and festival, war and law—all features of human culture long formed by play—as scientific and technological advances began to reshape worldviews and cultural imagination. Play no longer seemed to have any role in the serious running of the world. As we recall John Hughes's term, here the "Spirit of Utility" was born not just in the minds of philosophers and economists but also industrialists.[24] Everything now was to be useful, everything for profit. Utility now governed play, no longer the primeval, mystical pleasures of contemplation. Hence the rise of modern sports, with its organization and regimentation, where

20. Rahner, *Man at Play*, 10.
21. Rahner, *Man at Play*, 38.
22. Rahner, *Man at Play*, 85.
23. Huizinga, *Homo Ludens*, 192.
24. Hughes, *End of Work*, 217.

for a time the "play-element" found refuge but which ultimately was transformed into something it wasn't previously—an instrumentalized, segregated activity that one now had to make sense of as a means to an end. Play could no longer simply be fun or ritually serious, shaping culture inadvertently as it had in the past. Play now had to be *for* something, like training laborers or giving children a good shot at the best college. Play now served work, becoming itself a kind of work. Here began the developmental myth of youth sports and eventually their professionalization. Huizinga called it instead the *profanation* of play, a cultural wound.[25] Josef Pieper suggested it was also a human wound. The reason Pieper argued we should retain the ancient order of things—that the goal of work is leisure—is that to reverse it—that is, to make work the goal of leisure—would render us less human.[26] Pieper here stands with Saint Thomas and Aristotle and the others we've already encountered to argue that we are at our most human when we allow our intellects the leisure of contemplation—contemplation abdicated when leisure is destroyed by being made to serve other ends.[27] For instance, why go on vacation? To live life fully or to rest up for work? Why allow our kids to play? To have fun or to make the "elite" team so that they get into a good school so that they get a good job so that they have the best shot at running the same gauntlet all over again with their own kids? This subtle shift, this demotion of leisure and play—putting leisure and play to work—is *the* wound, the root cause of all our rushing around, our anxiety and restlessness, and our weary, all too modern subhumanity.

It's also a spiritual wound. Seeing it in myself, in my family and friends, as well as in ministry, it is clear what we have ruined: play. Allowed to become something it wasn't meant to be, an instrument to achieve lesser ends, youth sports no longer belong to leisure, no longer to contemplation, no longer to the freeing joy of play for play's sake. Rather, it belongs to work, to the rat race, to social reproduction. Which has made a thing like youth sports not

25. Huizinga, *Homo Ludens*, 196–98.
26. Pieper, *Leisure*, 42–44.
27. Pieper, *Leisure*, 27.

only a contributor to our uniquely modern, hurried anxiety but also to the loss of the spiritual rest Christ offers (Matt 11:28). Here we can imagine again a modern Sunday Christ—not, of course, how we've wounded him but how we've wounded ourselves by wounding our relationship with the only one who can give the genuine rest that keeps us human.

If this then is the wound of youth sports, how is it healed? As I said, to suggest Christians keep away from youth sports would be not only impossible but also fundamentally un-Christian. What then? To redeem youth sports, we must recover play. Christians should grasp the deeper reasons for this, that this is a moral ought not just "given the science" but also given the soul. Such redemption is twofold, involving first a challenge to the individual conscience and then a challenge to the "social structures" shaping youth sports today. Individually, it is a matter of vision and courage. Seeing what's a stake—the rest God gives in Christ, the good of our souls—the Christian should find the strength to stand up against a culture deceptively benign and profoundly at odds with happiness and holiness. As King and Starbuck put it, "It is up to us to decide whether we'll use sports or be used by them." If Christ is truly Lord of our lives, then at times we must decide to be different. There is indeed often something *contra mundum* about being a Christian. We should remember that, embrace it. Again, as King and Starbuck put it, "followers of Christ will sometimes make choices that are different from the ones those around us are making." This is where it begins: with you and me and with the pointedly personal question each of us should ask ourselves about whether we have the spiritual guts to resist being conformed to this age (Rom 12:2).

But what about challenging "social structures"? Here the Church and organizations such as the Aspen Institute's Sports and Society Program agree. Both seek to increase participation and inclusion in youth sports. The Aspen Institute, for instance, urges coaches to avoid cutting kids, to add teams instead. They also call on communities to support after-school programs for kids, for churches and other faith communities to help create opportunities

Why Sunday Matters

and eliminate the barriers to play that many children face, poorer children especially. They also insist organizations and teams stop using words like "elite" to describe children's sports. "No child qualifies as elite before growing into their body."[28] The Church agrees with this and has done since Pope Pius XII.[29] Sports should be part of a true "culture of encounter." Those involved in sports, especially organizations and leaders, should "reject a throwaway culture" and instead be "open, welcoming and inclusive." The Church wants everybody to play. The dicastery document, *Giving the Best of Yourself*, calls for sports in seminaries, for example; it even calls for parishes to promote and organize sports not only for young parishioners but the elderly too.[30] The Aspen Institute recommends organizations and other institutions embrace a model of youth sports that doesn't just prioritize performance, or discovering the best athletes destined for college or professional sports, but a model that offers each child the opportunity to become "physically literate by age 12."[31] This too fits with the Church's understanding of sports as something "aimed at the integral formation of the person," seeing sports truly in terms of education.[32] Youth sports are not the minor leagues of anything. They are games children play because play belongs to what it means to be human, what it means to grow and flourish in body and soul. Here the Church and the best of the world of sports agree, and it's what Christian leaders and organizations should be doing, working toward a more inclusive and more human vision of youth sports.

And it's a vision that necessarily includes Sunday, that understands, cherishes, and serves what Sunday is. Here the Church stands alone to offer wisdom as ancient and holy as the Sabbath itself. Speaking to athletes in the early 1950s, Pope Pius XII put it

---

28. Aspen Institute Sports and Society Program, "Sport for All, Play for Life: A Playbook to Get Every Kid in the Game," 32.
29. See Lixey et al., *Sport and Christianity*, 104–55.
30. Dicastery for Laity, Family and Life, *Giving the Best of Yourself* 5.3–5.5.
31. Aspen Institute Sports and Society Program, "Sport for All, Play for Life: A Playbook to Get Every Kid in the Game," 8.
32. Dicastery for Laity, Family and Life, *Giving the Best of Yourself* 5.3.

bluntly: "Do you wish to act rightly in gymnastics and sport? Then keep the Commandments." He insisted that athletes "keep the Lord's day holy, since sport does not excuse us from the discharge of our religious duties."[33] Pope Benedict XVI later talked about protecting and developing a "culture of Sunday." What he meant is that Christians should "preserve" Sunday as a day that frees us to remember that "our life is more a gift than an achievement."[34] He saw Sunday as a day we needed so as to resist the dehumanizing tyranny of totalizing work, the degradation of the rat race. The way Pope Saint John Paul II put it is that the life of sports and the spiritual and religious life, each with its obligations and discipline, should not be opposed but rather "harmonized."[35] One should not replace or eliminate the other; sports should not become a religion nor should religion seek to do away with sports. Rather, what such harmonization looks like is a community of families sharing together a rhythm of worship and play, a rhythm ultimately tying the community closer together. It's a vision put forward in *Giving the Best of Yourself*:

> If sport runs the risk of being the occasion to divide a family and to diminish the sanctity of Sunday as a holy day to uphold, it also can help integrate a family with other families in the celebration of Sunday, not only in the liturgy but in the life of the community. This does not mean that sports matches should not take place on Sundays, but rather, such events must not excuse families from attending Mass and should also promote the life of the family within community.[36]

The ideal is a disciplined harmony of play and worship. The vision is of a community of families living this harmony together. But, to be clear, this is not merely an appeal for Sunday attendance. Talking about this to a friend of mine, a monk and teacher, his response was simply, "Go to Mass!" Now, practically, that is solid

---

33. Lixey et al., *Sport and Christianity*, 116.
34. Lixey et al., *Sport and Christianity*, 231.
35. Lixey et al., *Sport and Christianity*, 127.
36. Dicastery for Laity, Family and Life, *Giving the Best of Yourself* 5.3.

Why Sunday Matters

Catholic advice, but there is more to it than that, something deeper. What we've been talking about all along is the human and spiritual good of play and the human and spiritual tragedy that comes with ruined play. The reason Sunday matters in all this, the reason the Church insists Mass be part of each Catholic family's Sunday, no matter how many teams you're on or games or tournaments you have scheduled, is that liturgy is itself play. Liturgy too is without purpose. Like contemplation, liturgy is a kind of playing before God. As to any game belongs its own world—its rules and boundaries—so too for the liturgy. This was Romano Guardini's insight, that the genius of the liturgy is that "it simply creates an entire spiritual world in which the soul can live according to the requirements of its nature."[37] Liturgy is play. It constructs for the worshiper another world, a fleetingly sacramental other world. As Heschel called the Sabbath a "palace in time," so too is Christian liturgy.[38] Liturgy plays a sacramental world into brief existence, all for the sake of rest, so that God may grant his people the rest they need as they make their way to heaven. That's why the Christian obligation to attend Sunday Mass is not merely an appeal for attendance. Here we see better the whole, the Church's deeper vision for things like youth sports, play, and worship. The Church believes that all of it approximates the rest God has always offered his people, but only when it is lived in harmony. Youth sports should serve the human person, helping each child to become someone who knows, loves, and worships God because that's what it means to be human, to flourish, and to find holiness. Play and worship are those gifts of creation that not only offer the pleasantness of rest but also a foretaste of heavenly rest. Play and worship mystically mirror each other. That's why the Church doesn't let families off the hook for Sunday Mass. The Church does not forbid games on Sunday, but the Church does insist upon Sunday Mass. Because as humans and children of God, we need that rest. That's why the Church insists Christian parents are still called to be Christians as they parent their children through the fun but sometimes dangerous world of

---

37. Guardini, *Spirit of Liturgy*, 56.
38. Heschel, *Sabbath*, 15.

youth sports. Because God made them parents precisely so that they might share his divine rest with their children. Because that is a Christian parent's most important job.

It should all fit together: youth sports, play, and worship. Conflict is only a matter of illusion and sin. But what practically does this harmony look like? What should Christian parents and Christian organizations do or stop doing? Aristotle said that what did the Spartans in was their failure to understand and embrace leisure. Perhaps we should learn from Aristotle's warning.[39] Perhaps we should also learn from our medieval ancestors who played lazily in the fields outside parish churches after Mass each Sunday or who gathered on the church porch to tell jokes and play games.[40] Perhaps bishops and priests should play games together at Christmas and Easter as they used to do.[41] Maybe the Church should make more space for free play. Perhaps parishes could make room for casual gatherings on occasional Sunday afternoons for no other purpose than to play, talk, laugh; to offer a space for friends and families to do nothing other than while away the time. Maybe we should also change the way we think about organized sports. Maybe Catholic schools and Catholic sports leagues should lead the way. Maybe putting a young kid on an "elite" competitive travel lacrosse team is not a good idea. Maybe a kid playing three soccer games in one day is a bad idea. Maybe we need to talk about this stuff candidly, charitably. Maybe Catholic schools and parishes, parents, coaches, and clergy should talk about it and then rethink their sports programs. Are they organized to include or exclude? Do Catholic sports programs cherish Sunday worship or pull families away from Mass? Do they contribute to a Sunday culture—one more playful, more holy? When are practices scheduled and games played? And do they value performance over participation? What does playing time look like for each child? Are youth sports programs too competitive too early? Again, the Church wants more play not less. The vision of the Church is decidedly

---

39. Aristotle, *Politics* 1269a, 1338b.
40. Ratzinger, *Behold the Pierced One*, 119.
41. Rahner, *Man at Play*, 84.

not elitist. This is the sort of examination of conscience we Christian parents, clergy, coaches, and administrators must undertake. These are the wounds that must be healed. What the renewal of youth sports looks like is uncertain, but it will certainly lead to youth sports that look far different than they do today. But first it's up to those of us called to raise our children together in the midst of the Church, those courageous enough to remember their vocation and responsibility to share God's rest with their children, to dare to be different.

4

The Poor and Work, or Why We Cannot See the Sabbath

> The Church in fact is the formal religion of the rich. It is therefore nothing; that is why it means nothing.
>
> —Charles Péguy

At times of necessity in vestments of work the faithful come to Mass. To the early Mass, sometimes the late, they come recognizably dressed. A nurse in scrubs, a business traveler with carry-on in tow, a police officer just off duty: they are easy to spot among the retired and the young families up early, the kids drowsy in their jerseys ready for the game. In our parish there's a piano player, often in his tuxedo not yet buttoned up. I enjoy seeing him, exchanging smiles and sacraments as he makes his way to play somewhere. The Mass must be how he begins his music. I also enjoy our comedian, sometimes dressed for his show, his mismatched leopard print boots and sequined jacket, which I am sure makes other parishioners wonder just what he's on about. But I know him, and he makes me think of the laughter of heaven.

Why Sunday Matters

The working world is reflected upon the sacrifice. It is possible to see it, but it takes a trained eye, a spiritual sort of seeing. *Discerning the body* is how Saint Paul put it. It's a task, he frighteningly warned, that makes or breaks the Eucharist (1 Cor 11:28).

Another person, hardly noticed, challenges me to see even more of the world mirrored in the Mass. A Black woman, small in stature, when she comes to Mass, she's dressed for the warehouse—shorts and T-shirt, sneakers, a headscarf. Her smile is the crown of her beauty. Normally she leaves Mass early, which normally irritates me but not when she does it. Speaking to her one morning, I asked her name, how she was, what she did for work. I told her it was good to see her. She told me she worked in an Amazon fulfillment center. Whenever at Mass, she was either on her way to work or from it. She tried never to miss Sunday Mass. "I always want to thank my Lord," she told me with a smile as she rushed out the door, the Mass now reflected upon the world through her.

But as I said, she challenges me, by her smallest kindness, to see the gathered congregation differently. She reminds me that I should see them, that I should know them, that we gathered in Christ should know each other. Which is particularly difficult today, especially in a large parish like the one I serve. Collected as individuals in our pews as customers more than communicants, today we are more likely to treat our parishes like fast-food franchises, sacrament centers managed for mass convenience, rather than as organic communities. Many of us are so hidden within the masses of the Mass as to be almost invisible. It is hard to see one another when, due to culture and conditioning, some don't want to see, and others don't want to be seen. And although our mutual invisibility isn't inevitable, even the smallest act of hospitality or a single glance can change it, still it often seems impossible for us to see each other.

And this, of course, is doubly true of the poor and the marginalized. In many places of the Church today they are quite difficult to see. For instance, the parish I serve is wonderful; it's diverse, joyful, faithful, welcoming. But it's also affluent, and sometimes our affluence makes non-affluence hard to see. It's not impossible.

The Poor and Work, or Why We Cannot See the Sabbath

My sister the Amazon employee caught my eye, my ear, and my heart, but that's an experience far too sentimental, too rare in my parish. But I am not picking on my own community. What is true of my parish is true of others. Many Christian communities are segregated in more ways than one. Martin Luther King Jr. said long ago that 11:00 a.m. on Sunday was the most racially segregated hour in America, and that likely remains the case. But it's also true that we have in our churches long been economically segregated, the rich cloistered away from the poor.[1] Yet this wasn't always so.

There was a time when Christians saw the poor more clearly, more closely than we do today. Flannery O'Connor wrote once, "You hear of the Poor, but you seldom see them."[2] Again, this wasn't always true. A profound yet forgotten difference marks our contemporary experience of churchgoing from the past. Today what's different is that we no longer encounter the poor. Or, if we do, it's a rare, uncomfortable experience, a matter for either the usher, for security, or even the pastor, to handle discreetly. For many of us today the poor are no longer part of our normal churchgoing experience. But, as I said, once upon a time, this wasn't the case. In the past, poverty was everywhere a more visible reality than it is today in the developed world. This was true of churchgoing too. To go to Mass a thousand years ago, one had to enter doors surrounded by beggars, by the poor huddled within the porches of the church. The poor were always on the move from church to church, from feast to feast, funeral to funeral, and even wedding to wedding, because at each of these gatherings the poor were sure to be recognized, integrated, and given some measure of alms.[3] Because in the past the role of the poor, the beggar, was visibly social and even liturgical.

At the shrine of Saint Martin of Tours in the sixth century, for example, it would have been unthinkable to enter without first giving alms to the *matricularii*, officially sanctioned beggars

---

1. King, *Knock at Midnight*, 146.
2. O'Connor, *Habit of Being*, 487.
3. Geremek, *Poverty*, 39.

loitering about the entrance.[4] In the Middle Ages the poor were often integrated ceremonially into the daily rituals of monastic communities. The *mandatum*, for instance, the ritual washing of feet, in some monasteries was done frequently, sometimes daily. Several beggars, selected in advance by either the porter or the almoner, would stand before each monk who, at the ringing of a bell, would kneel before "Christ in His poor" then wash and kiss the beggar's feet.[5] At funerals it was also common practice to make provision for the poor to attend in order to pray and visibly mourn the deceased. Thomas Snellyng, for example, a sixteenth-century Norwich butcher, paid a penny apiece to eighteen poor men to carry candles about his hearse. They were also invited along with the rest of the parish to a dinner after the funeral at which each poor person present received a small loaf of bread.[6] Examples of such acts of charity abound throughout Christian history, practices that today have almost entirely disappeared.

None of these forgotten charitable practices were efficient. They were never meant to eliminate poverty. As the biblical theologian Gary Anderson puts it, "To think of poverty as a social problem that could be solved was not really imaginable in the mindset of premodern man."[7] Visibly incorporating the poor into the ceremonies of society was a matter of charitable performance. It displayed the bonds that existed between the rich and the poor. This was not, however, mere ostentation or hypocrisy. Rather, it was the logical outworking of the theological features of a Christian social imagination that was once universal. Peter Brown, in several places, has described this transformation of social imagination from Greek and Roman notions of civic benefaction to a more explicitly Jewish and Christian idea of a society formed by the charitable ordering of the rich to the poor. In late antiquity, before the rise of Christianity, the imagined recipients of alms were members of a particular civic community. To be eligible for alms

---

4. Brown, *Through the Eye of a Needle*, 510–13.
5. Mollat, *Poor in the Middle Ages*, 49.
6. Maddern, "Market for Charitable Performances?," 91.
7. Anderson, *Charity*, 8.

The Poor and Work, or Why We Cannot See the Sabbath

one had first to belong to the polis. After the social rise of Christianity, however, the recipients of alms belonged to a broader, more ecclesiastically integrated category of persons simply understood as God's poor.[8] The Church, beginning in the fourth century, as it began slowly to shape social imagination, imported not only its ancient biblical charitable practices into wider society but also its way of thinking about the poor. The relationship between the rich and the poor changed from a civic relationship into a sacred one. Now the poor were bound to the rich not just by virtue of belonging to the polis but also in a relationship of charity established by God himself, and in such a way that both the rich and the poor had recognizable roles to play—the rich to give and the poor to receive and pray. As described in the seventh-century *Life of St. Eligius*, "God could have made all men rich, but He wanted there to be poor people in this world, that the rich might be able to redeem their sins."[9] That was the sacred bond. Rich and poor needed each other both materially and spiritually. This is not how we think today. Even many Christians today would find this a problematic ordering of the poor to the rich. Yet that is how for many centuries the relationship of the rich to the poor was conceived, and not without good social effect.

For such theological imagination to have been social, it had to be visible. That's why Christians used to invite the poor to weddings and funerals, why they would never have called the police if beggars showed up to Mass. Underneath these diverse and sometimes curious, now extinct, charitable practices was the habit of seeing the poor. Such habits, encouraged in the Gospels—"Lord, when did we see you hungry and feed you, or thirsty and give you drink?" (Matt 25:37)—were constantly extolled in early Christian preaching. In his sermons on Lazarus and the rich man, for instance, Saint John Chrysostom repeatedly exhorted his listeners to see the rich and the poor differently, that is, in the light of eternity. "Let us not regard what is present, but consider what is to come. Let us examine not the outer garments but the conscience of each

---

8. Brown, *Poverty and Leadership in the Later Roman Empire*, 3–5, 74–80.
9. Geremek, *Poverty*, 20.

person," he said. It was equally a mistake to think the poor were judged by God as it was to think the rich were blessed, for only in heaven would the full truth of things be revealed. "Therefore," Chrysostom said, "when you see anyone living in wickedness but suffering no misfortune in this life do not call him lucky, but weep for him and mourn for him, because he will have to endure all the misfortunes in the next life." Likewise, "when you see anyone cultivating virtue, but enduring a multitude of trials, call him lucky, envy him, because all his sins are being dissolved in this life, and a great reward for his endurance is being prepared in the next life."[10] But it wasn't just a matter of seeing the poor in the light of eternity. It was first a matter of seeing the poor themselves.

Such was the thrust of the preaching of the Cappadocians, for instance, Saint Basil the Great and Saint Gregory Nazianzen especially.[11] Preaching in times of famine and disease, Saint Basil and Saint Gregory forcefully put before their listeners the sufferings of the famished and the leprous chiefly so that they would see them. "How can I bring the sufferings of the poverty-stricken to your attention?" Saint Basil asked.[12] To help their people see the poor, at times Saint Basil's and Saint Gregory's preaching were intentionally grotesque. As when Saint Basil described the effects of starvation, he did so precisely to disturb:

> The body becomes dehydrated, its temperature drops, its bulk dwindles, its strength passes away. Skin clings to bone like a spider's web. The flesh loses its natural coloration: its ruddiness fades as the flow of blood decreases, while the alabaster of the skin turns discolored and dark. The body takes on a mottled hue, with yellow and black patches mingling in a terrible manner to see. The knees can no longer support the weight of the body, but are forced to drag along behind. The voice grows weak and feeble. The eyes become diseased and are rendered useless, sunken in their sockets like fruits that shrivel up their skins. The belly is empty, shrunken to nothingness,

10. Chrysostom, *On Wealth and Poverty*, 37, 63.
11. See Holman, *Hungry Are Dying*.
12. "I Will Tear Down My Barns," in Basil, *On Social Justice*, 64.

The Poor and Work, or Why We Cannot See the Sabbath

> possessing neither girth nor the natural tone of the bowels, so that the bones of the spine are visible from the front.[13]

Or, as when Saint Gregory Nazianzen preached about the sufferings of lepers, he was equally set on upsetting his listeners:

> There lies before our eyes a dreadful and pathetic sight, one that no one would believe who has not seen it: human beings alive yet dead, disfigured in almost every part of their bodies, barely recognizable for who they once were or where they came from; or rather, the pitiful wreckage of what had once been human beings. By way of identification they keep calling out the names of their mothers and fathers, brothers, and places or origin: "I am the son of so-and-so. So-and-so is my mother. This is my name. You used to be a close friend of mine." And this they do because they cannot be identified from the way they used to look.[14]

The point of such preaching was not simply to make their listeners feel so guilty that they would donate to works and institutions of charity—although that was certainly an objective—rather, it was to train Christians to see the world, and both the poor and the rich in it, differently. Their goal was to reinforce the teaching of Matthew's Gospel, that Jesus Christ is to be seen in the poor—"these, our brothers in God, whether you like it or not," Saint Gregory said.[15] That's why, he said, "I stand in terror of his left hand and the goats." For he knew, as he tried to warn his people, that those to be condemned, as foretold in the parable, were those who "did not serve Christ through the poor."[16] For they never learned how to see Jesus in them. Because they refused even to look.

But again, it's important to remember that this is a habit of seeing born within visible precincts of the sacred, as mentioned before, in places like shrines and monasteries and parishes. That

---

13. "In Time of Famine and Drought," in Basil, *On Social Justice*, 84.
14. Gregory of Nazianzus, *Select Orations*, 14.10.
15. Gregory of Nazianzus, *Select Orations*, 14.14.
16. Gregory of Nazianzus, *Select Orations*, 14.39.

is, sacred sites were the places Christians—sometimes painfully—learned how to see the poor. It isn't accidental, for instance, that Saint Gregory Nazianzen rhetorically placed next to one another the cries of the poor and the cries of worship:

> Who is not overcome as their plaintive cries rise in a symphony of lament? What ear can bear the sound? What eye can take the sight? They lie beside one another, a wretched union born of disease, each contributing his own misfortune to the common fund of misery, thus heightening each other's distress; pitiful in their affliction, more so in the sharing of it. Some bystanders gather round them like spectators at a drama, deeply affected, but only for a moment. In the hot sun and the dust they writhe at men's feet; and sometimes, too, they are tormented by biting cold and rain and blasts of wind and narrowly escape being trampled on only because we find it repugnant to come into contact with them. Their mournful pleas stand in jarring contrast to the sacred chanting within and their piteous lament forms a counterpoint to the mystic voices.[17]

Saint Gregory wanted to make the poor visible in sacred space, to train his people to see the poor they would inevitably encounter as they went about the practice of their religion. He wanted them to see the poor not as obstacles to be dodged but as Christ to be adored and served. His point was to preserve religion as a matter of justice.

But seeing the poor this way would disappear over time. The strange practices of visible charity would eventually fade away. How this happened is its own long story that we needn't detail here. Population growth in the Middle Ages and urbanization, among other things, worked to refashion the image of the poor in popular imagination. Although the idea of God's poor remained—although often conflated with clergy, religious, mendicants and other "voluntary poor"—more and more it was eclipsed by the idea of the poor as vagrants, criminals, and vectors of disease.[18]

---

17. Gregory of Nazianzus, *Select Orations*, 14.13.
18. Mollat, *Poor in the Middle Ages*, 226; Geremek, *Poverty*, 127.

The Poor and Work, or Why We Cannot See the Sabbath

The poor were no longer thought to play a role in the social order of charity; rather, they became a problem to be managed. By the sixteenth century, poverty had become an evil to be eliminated. Poor laws outlawing public begging emerged in both Protestant and Catholic Europe.[19] Although there was in some corners of the Catholic world significant resistance to these shifting attitudes and new laws that restricted begging, the larger shift in social imagination was inevitable.[20] Domingo de Soto, for instance, a sixteenth-century Dominican, despised the new poor laws. "Truly, the saints would have thought these laws were only laid down out of hatred for a class that actually deserves pity," he wrote.[21] For De Soto these laws contradicted both natural and divine law. Yet even among Catholics, De Soto's argument didn't win the day. The poor were more a population to be managed; poverty was a blight to be cleared, not ritually integrated. This was not an entirely lamentable change, for it did bring about modern scientific and political efforts to eliminate poverty on a wide scale; such a thing was just never imagined in premodern times. Yet, at the same time something good was lost; as Michel Mollat put it, "poverty lost its sacred status."[22] Christians saw the poor differently, and in time they would no longer see the poor at all, at least not in the churches. Well into modernity, as efforts to eliminate poverty were organized, churches and parishes remained logistically involved. In fact, the modern structures and practices of organized charity were built upon the foundations churches had already built.[23] However, over time the structures and practices of such charity migrated from places of worship. Churches eventually became places where the poor were *not* seen, nor did anyone want to see the poor in places of worship anymore. The poor no longer belonged in the churches, only the rich, or at least the non-poor. Sixteenth-century Venetian historian Marino Sanudo represents this new mentality, this new

---

19. Farmer, "From Personal Charity to Centralised Poor Relief," 20–21.
20. Geremek, *Poverty*, 140–41, 189.
21. Soto, *Deliberation on the Cause of the Poor*, 51.
22. Mollat, *Poor in the Middle Ages*, 256.
23. Farmer, "From Personal Charity to Centralised Poor Relief," 28.

aversion to the poor present within the precincts of the sacred: "Impossible to listen to mass in peace, for at least a dozen beggars will surround you; impossible to open your purse without an immediate plea for money," he wrote, obviously irritated, in 1527.[24] In time, more and more Christians would think about the poor just like this—the way most of us think of the poor now.

But why spend so much time talking about how Christians today see the poor differently? Because what I ultimately want to talk about is work and the Sabbath. For it is precisely the fact that we see the poor differently—or, more precisely still, that we no longer see them at all—that makes what is often said about Christians and Sunday now utterly meaningless. Remember from the first chapter that, biblically speaking, the Sabbath and justice are inseparably linked. Or one could put it, the Sabbath is fundamentally a rite of justice. Because God liberated the Hebrews from Egypt, he commanded Sabbath observance (Deut 5:15). Thus, to practice liberation is always in some way to practice the Sabbath, especially when it's a matter of liberating the poor. That's what makes for a Sabbath in which God delights: to break bread with the hungry, to welcome the homeless into one's home, not hiding from the poor, but instead seeing them (Isa 58:6-7, 13). It is when we fail to see the poor, as both Isaiah and Amos attest, that our Sabbaths become something God hates (Isa 1:13-14; Amos 5:20-21). When injustice covered in luxury "forces the lowly out of the way," our religion becomes not simply unreal, it becomes detestable (Amos 2:7). That is why to say anything meaningful at all about the relation of work to the Sabbath we must first remember this more fundamental relation of justice to the Sabbath. Which we can only accomplish by recovering earlier Christian habits of seeing the poor. Otherwise, as often is the case, whatever we say about work and the Sabbath becomes only a privileged discussion about work-life balance, something better suited to life coaches and other purveyors of that particularly modern commodity we call "wellness." Which is something, of course, different than holiness, not the Sabbath's real substance (Exod 20:8).

24. Geremek, *Poverty*, 132.

The Poor and Work, or Why We Cannot See the Sabbath

Learning to see the poorer among us, to recover this primitive Christian habit, is precisely what our recent popes have asked us to do. Repeatedly has Pope Francis urged everyone—but especially those of us in the developed world, and even more especially those of us who by one relative measure or another can be called rich—to regain the capacity to see more fully both creation and creatures. He invites us to see the world mystically, borrowing the "gaze of Jesus," a way of seeing that is "attentive to the beauty that there is in the world," no longer seeing the world and its inhabitants "under merely natural guise."[25] It's a way of seeing many may assume we have lost. Pope Francis points to contradictions evident in the contrast between what we say about ourselves and the way we act. For instance, some may understandably conclude the equal dignity "solemnly proclaimed" in such weighty documents as The Universal Declaration of Human Rights is far from "truly recognized, respected, protected and promoted in every situation."[26] Fundamentally a failure of recognition, of sight, it's why Pope Francis insists we recover "a gaze transformed by charity."[27] But that is precisely what's so difficult—and here Pope Francis, Pope Benedict XVI, and Pope Saint John Paul II (and others) are in perfect harmony—because on a massive scale billions of us have been conditioned in such a way, our consciences dulled to such an extent, that we "can no longer distinguish what is human."[28] We have in many ways become at the same time both agents and victims of a "practical atheism," pushers and addicts of a reductive, purely materialist understanding or ourselves and others.[29] Saint Pope John Paul II talked about the "eclipse of God and man"—again, imagery related to our capacity to see—which, in the aggregate creates and recreates what he repeatedly called "structures of sin."[30] This language of structures is simply a way to describe the "sum

25. Francis, *Laudato Si'* 97, 100.
26. Francis, *Fratelli Tutti*, 22.
27. Francis, *Fratelli Tutti*, 187.
28. Benedict XVI, *Caritas in Veritate*, 75.
29. Benedict XVI, *Caritas in Veritate*, 29.
30. John Paul II, *Evangelium Vitae*, 11–12, 21–24, 59.

total of negative factors" creating what from a Christian standpoint is a perverse social imagination, perverse in that it blinds us to the victims of the social and economic order, that is, the poor and marginalized.[31] This is why, compared to earlier Christians, our moral capacity to see to the poor is markedly clouded. We have been rendered deaf and blind by our prosperity. "While the poor of the world continue knocking on the doors of the rich," Pope Benedict XVI warned, "the world of affluence runs the risk of no longer hearing those knocks."[32] Pope Francis writes of a blinding narcissism born of affluence: "caught up with our own needs, the sight of a person who is suffering disturbs us," conditioned as we are by a "society that seeks prosperity but turns its back on suffering."[33] And failing to see the poor, we are habituated to loneliness; which, on the personal level tempts us "to confuse happiness and salvation with immanent forms of material prosperity."[34] We begin to seek a purely materialist, purely individualistic salvation, which—not only is it to enter a death spiral of despair—inevitably erodes all social bonds.[35] No matter how many socio-economically identical friends we have, we begin to lose a "sense of belonging to a single human family," growing indifferent to one another. The effect in the aggregate, by means of eroded solidarity, is the advent of the "culture of death," the relentless war of the strong against the weak.[36] Pope Saint John Paul II pointed to our blindness to the unborn and other marginalized and vulnerable persons. Pope Francis builds on this, arguing we are also blind to the victims of the global economy. "Some parts of our human family, it appears, can be readily sacrificed for the sake of others considered worthy of a carefree existence," he suggests.[37] Such is our collective blindness and its brutal effects, that although we live in a beautiful world, we

31. John Paul II, *Sollicitudo rei socialis*, 36.
32. Benedict XVI, *Caritas in Veritate*, 75.
33. Francis, *Frattelli Tutti*, 65.
34. Benedict XVI, *Caritas in Veritate*, 34.
35. John Paul II, *Evangelium Vitae*, 19–20.
36. John Paul II, *Evangelium Vitae*, 19–20.
37. Francis, *Fratelli Tutti*, 18.

The Poor and Work, or Why We Cannot See the Sabbath

fail to see what's wicked about it. It's as the imprisoned Fr. Sebastian reflected, thinking on the guards indifferent to his plight, in Shūsaku Endō's novel *Silence*: "Sin is for one man to walk brutally over the life of another and to be quite oblivious of the wounds he has left behind."[38] Such is what we must recognize about ourselves if we're to recover any proper understanding of our work's relation to the Sabbath, how we have sinned against not only God but each other too, especially those we are in the habit of ignoring.

But how do we do that? Ultimately, as Pope Francis adamantly teaches, we must learn to listen to the poor and the marginalized themselves.[39] We would also do well to make ourselves students of the journalists, social scientists, and scholars who work to uncover the unpleasant hidden realities of our beautiful world. Decades ago, Michael Harrington wrote about the "other America, the America of poverty." It's an America "hidden today in a way that it never was before." This remains true today. And it's also still true, as Harrington said, that "it takes an effort of the intellect and will even to see them."[40] They are who we must take care to see: the poor within the world we have made.

Take, for example, what's hidden within and by our habits of consumption. As Ivan Illich said once, "Almost everyone in rich societies is a destructive consumer."[41] From Saint Pope John Paul II to Pope Francis, papal warnings about the sin and effects of overconsumption have only increased. "Man often seems to see no other meaning in his natural environment than what serves for immediate use and consumption," Saint Pope John Paul II said at the beginning of his pontificate.[42] By Pope Francis's pontificate this warning had become only more urgent: "Doomsday predictions can no longer be met with irony or disdain. We may well be leaving to coming generations debris, desolation and filth. The place of consumption, waste, and environmental change has so stretched

38. Endō, *Silence*, 92.
39. Francis, *Fratelli Tutti*, 233–35.
40. Harrington, *Other America*, 2–3.
41. Illich, *Tools for Conviviality*, 102.
42. John Paul II, *Redemptor Hominis*, 15.

the planet's capacity that our contemporary lifestyle, unsustainable as it is, can only precipitate catastrophes, such as those which even now periodically occur in different areas of the world."[43] We are caught seemingly in a trap of addictive consumption on a global scale. As J. B. MacKinnon begins in his book *The Day the World Stops Shopping*, "The twenty-first century has brought a critical dilemma into sharp relief: we must stop shopping, and yet we can't stop shopping." And it is we, the rich, who do most of the consuming. "The average person in a rich country consumes thirteen times as much as the average person in a poor one," MacKinnon continues.[44] If every person on the planet, for instance, lived like ordinary Americans, "we would need five Earths' worth of resources to sustain our lifestyles." It's an addiction supported by hyper-efficient business models that fit hand-in-glove within economic systems unmoored from morality. Hence the Church's longstanding criticism of impersonal, morally unguided capitalism which the Church has consistently twinned with its criticism of communism.[45] To apply only "commercial logic" to economic activity (Saint Pope John Paul II spoke of "economism"), to think of economics "merely as an engine for wealth creation," is immoral, Pope Benedict XVI taught.[46] Because it rejects the moral priority of the human person.[47] But what does this look like in practice? And how are we implicated? We are caught within this immoral structure precisely because we are addicted to consumption. It is because, although we hardly suspect it, one of the most immoral things about us is that we are Amazon and Walmart customers addicted to cheap clothes and cheap food. We demand an economic system that must by its very design exploit both the environment and the poor. Again, from Saint Pope John Paul II to Pope Francis, the modern papacy has repeatedly criticized business models

43. Francis, *Laudato Si'* 161.

44. MacKinnon, *Day the World Stops Shopping*, 6.

45. John Paul II, *Laborem Exercens*, 14.

46. Benedict XVI, *Caritas in Veritate*, 36; John Paul II, *Laborem Exercens*, 13.

47. John Paul II, *Laborem Exercens*, 12.

obsessed "with reducing labor costs with no concern for its grave consequences."[48] Such business models are designed only to maximize profits for investors and are operated by a "cosmopolitan class of managers" who are "answerable only to the shareholders."[49] This constitutes a denial of the common good; and again, the immorality of it is ours as consumers of these convenient goods.[50] As Genevieve LeBaron admits in her sobering book *Combatting Modern Slavery*, "the business of forced labor continues to boom in today's global economy." And further, "most of us still participate" in this economy that, LeBaron argues, depends on exploitation by design.[51] What Pope Benedict XVI wrote about "commercial logic" LeBaron calls the "financialization" of the global economy and global supply chains. Massive, passively managed, assets invested in multinational corporations, LeBaron argues, "is one of several factors pushing them towards prioritizing short-term financial gain and expansion."[52] And it's precisely this globalized profit motive that creates the fundamentally immoral supply chains that serve us. LeBaron connects the dots:

> Forced labour, and labour exploitation more broadly, does not occur randomly or spontaneously in global supply chains. Rather, it is a logical outcome of the way that contemporary supply chains are set up. The global retail production model characterized by low-cost, high volume and high-turnover goods triggers predictable business demand for forced labour and exploitation. Pressure on supplier firms to produce goods for very low prices in short time windows combine with broader political dynamics such as low levels of labour law enforcement and unionization to create a business climate in which suppliers can use forced labour as a strategy to

48. Francis, *Fratelli Tutti*, 20; see also John Paul II, *Laborem Exercens*, 17.
49. Benedict XVI, *Caritas in Veritate*, 40.
50. Benedict XVI, *Caritas in Veritate*, 21.
51. LeBaron, *Combatting Modern Slavery*, 38.
52. LeBaron, *Combatting Modern Slavery*, 69–70.

Why Sunday Matters

deliver orders and stay afloat in increasingly competitive markets.[53]

This is what's behind the ease of one-click shopping, our affordable clothes. And we keep buying more. As J. B. MacKinnon sums it up: "The number of garments sold each year has approximately doubled in just the last fifteen years. The number now exceeds one hundred billion, at about fifteen articles of clothing per year per person on the planet." Even though the clothes we buy are increasingly what MacKinnon calls "garbage-in-waiting," we just can't seem to get enough.[54] Yet the problem—again to quote MacKinnon—is that "if something's too cheap, somebody else is paying."[55] This is precisely what we do not see, what we do not want to see. We don't want to see what goes into the clothes we wear or the food we eat. Eyal Press calls it the "dirty work" of America. "The lifestyles of many Americans—the food we eat, the cars we drive—are sustained by dirty work," he argues. Looking just at America, this is the work, he suggests, we intentionally put out of sight today because, although we rely on it, we find it distasteful and morally suspect—for example, the work of prison guards, many social and mental health workers, meat packers and poultry plant workers. Alongside garment workers in places like Bangladesh, workers here in America are also "hidden, making it easier for 'good people' to avoid seeing or thinking about them."[56] Again, just like the modern papacy, Press suggests it's a matter of seeing. "The problem is not a dearth of information but the fact that many choose to avert their eyes, not only from dirty work but also from those who get stuck doing it, people with whom they almost never interact and find easy to judge."[57] People like my parishioner who works in an Amazon fulfillment center. I don't really know her; she belongs among the hidden essential workers who surround me, who

---

53. LeBaron, *Combatting Modern Slavery*, 44.
54. MacKinnon, *Day the World Stops Shopping*, 156.
55. MacKinnon, *Day the World Stops Shopping*, 159.
56. Press, *Dirty Work*, 12–13.
57. Press, *Dirty Work*, 269.

make my world work, the people Lawrence Wright calls "shadow people."[58] Yet I do have a hazy memory of buried headlines about poor working conditions in some of Amazon's fulfillment centers across America. Like the story from 2011 of workers passing out in a hot warehouse in Allentown, Pennsylvania: in his book *Fulfillment*, Alec MacGillis says, "the company had stationed medics outside to handle workers fainting from the heat instead of paying for air-conditioning."[59] I also faintly recall headlines about forces later detailed in MacGillis's book about how Amazon has gutted small businesses all across the country, replacing them with what, by plain reckoning, is a monopoly, re-employing those ousted from their erased businesses at fractions of their earlier wages.[60] All of these stories are hidden just underneath the surface of my beautiful world. They explain why my parishioner, a child of God and Amazon employee, was dressed differently, because of the hard work I give her with merely the swipe of a thumb across my phone. This is what I so often refuse to see, and it's what so often makes my sabbaths unreal.

Which brings us finally to the deeper problems of work and rest, labor and the Sabbath. Derek Thompson is correct. What he calls "workism" is indeed, among our new atheisms, "a kind of religion." "It is the belief that work is not only necessary to economic production, but also the centerpiece of one's identity and life's purpose."[61] The logic of the "rat race," the logic of "total work," isn't just economic. "It's emotional—even spiritual," Thompson writes. The educated and the rich work more today than ever before. "The best-educated and highest-earning Americans, who can have whatever they want, have chosen the office for the same reason that devout Christians attend church on Sundays: It's where they feel most themselves."[62] As Jonathan Malesic, in his book *The End of Burnout*, puts it, work has been transformed into a "spiritual

58. Press, *Dirty Work*, 157.
59. MacGillis, *Fulfillment*, 133.
60. MacGillis, *Fulfillment*, 162.
61. Thompson, *On Work*, 35.
62. Thompson, *On Work*, 37.

enterprise," something offering what work had never on its own supplied before—fulfillment.[63] This, of course, is fundamentally the Protestant ethos which Max Weber argued shaped the "spirit of capitalism." The idea that "the fulfilment of duty in worldly affairs" represents the "highest form which the moral activity of the individual could assume" is for Weber the culturally dominant understanding of work that Josef Pieper would later call "total work."[64] The "spirit of capitalism" is the antithesis of that ancient, more humane understanding of work as something that exists for the sake of the *vita contemplativa*.[65] This explains what Thompson calls the "cult of achievement," the effects of which we explored in our earlier chapters on youth sports but which touches everything in our society and culture, ruining leisure by reducing it to a means to an end. But, of course, today Weber's spirit of capitalism is no longer even Protestant, but rather degraded and secular.[66] Still trapped in what Malesic calls the "Calvinist cage," the immanent spiritual pragmatism of the early Reformers has given way to mere immanence. Yet still, as Thompson rightly insists, "everybody worships something."[67] Hence "workism" has become the sacrificial religion of the privileged guilty.

Which is why what Aldous Huxley said of present and future totalitarianisms isn't exactly correct. He said that people would come to "love their servitude."[68] That's not quite right. Rather, what we have constructed from the ruins of our post-Christian Weberian world is a new religion; we've attempted an atonement. We may not see the injustices of our effervescent world, we may not see the poor, but we know they exist. We feel it; even the half-humane are haunted by it. It is the existential aporia of the privileged, that modern concoction of anxiety and guilt we desperately want to escape. That's why we don't know what true Sabbath is anymore, why

---

63. Malesic, *End of Burnout*, 119.
64. Weber, *Protestant Ethic and the Spirit of Capitalism*, 40.
65. Pieper, *Leisure*, 21, 27.
66. Hughes, *End of Work*, 41.
67. Thompson, *On Work*, 35.
68. Huxley, *Brave New World*, xiv.

The Poor and Work, or Why We Cannot See the Sabbath

we know no genuine rest, why mere shallow exhortations to take it easy on Sunday, to go to Mass, are by themselves insufficient and at worst grotesque. Because the harshest judgments of the prophets still suit us. Instead of justice we've opted for sentimentality, moral therapeutic deism, and other technologies of the self. Which in the end does not work. But what then can we do? Is the Sabbath possible at all? Do we deserve it?

5

Discerning the Body and Seeing the Sabbath

... may you excel in this gracious act also.

—2 CORINTHIANS 8:7

AVARICE USED TO BOTHER preachers. Once upon a time, they even preached against it. The danger of usury, that child of avarice, was often woven into the warnings of the Church's fiercest preaching. As the towns and cities of Europe were born, as a new economics gave birth to a new kind of merchant, so did preachers' anxiety about the glittering yet sometimes wicked spiritual effects of it all. They feared religion was turning into a deceptive thing, evil despite appearances. Medieval exempla warning of the evils of greed and ill-gotten gains are as numerous as those praising the good of charity. Fantastic stories, legends, moralistic anecdotes telling how our deeds, be they evil or good, touch upon religious practice, fill medieval sermons. One such story from the fifteenth century, for example, tells of a known usurer who donated money for the building of a church. At the church's consecration, much to the

Discerning the Body and Seeing the Sabbath

shock of the faithful, the devil showed up. There to claim the building as his own, what was his by right, he said the church was his because it had been built with his profits.[1] Another story from the *exempla* of Jacques de Vitry tells of a noble woman who momentarily stepped out of church in the middle of Mass to offer some of her clothes to a poor woman she had noticed shivering in the belfry. The moment she stepped outside, the priest miraculously could no longer celebrate the Mass; he was frozen in the middle of his prayers, the story goes, until she returned.[2] A primitive warning these strange medieval stories offer regarding the hypocrisy or harmony of life and worship, such an admonishment doesn't trouble as much the modern soul. But our ancestors were different. In the medieval mind charity and wickedness bore immediately upon the sacred and upon ritual. And that's because the fears and hopes of our ancestors were still largely biblical.

It's a moral and spiritual connection we no longer recognize, how our work relates to our Sabbaths. The suspicion is that the former has possibly made the latter not just detestable, in the biblical sense, but also unreal. To think seriously about work and the Sabbath is not merely to rehash the privileged conflicts of work-life balance, it's to wrestle with the nauseating possibility that our religion is no longer real. Not that God is no longer real nor truth nor the faith, but maybe our living the faith isn't as real as we think it is. I use here the admittedly imprecise term *unreal* to underline what's potentially delusional in our thinking about things like the Sabbath, particularly when we've not thought about justice. "A believer may be untrue to everything that his faith demands of him, and yet think he is close to God and better than others," Pope Francis writes in *Fratelli Tutti*.[3] The warnings of the prophets are not out of date. It's a sobering truth unwelcome among the privileged, truth calling out the lie of our comfortable therapeutic deisms both Protestant and Catholic. Waiting for us like God at the judgment is the truth that we have forgotten how to see the

1. Rubin, *Charity and Community in Medieval Cambridge*, 89.
2. Vitry, *Exempla*, 93.
3. Francis, *Fratelli Tutti*, 74.

poor, that today we easily and elegantly shift our gaze.⁴ Because we have become like the Corinthians of old no longer able to discern the body (1 Cor 11:29).

Our first task then is to see the poor again, to return to the older, messier way Christians used to see them, to live with them, love them, and worship God with them—up close. When stuck in a blind alley, Peter Maurin wrote, "the only thing to do is go back."⁵ Undoubtedly good is the Church's vast philanthropic work, all those Catholic institutions fighting poverty all over the world or helping people in times of disaster. But we've lost too much, too many of us, daily intimacy with the poor. We must see Lazarus again (Luke 16:19–31). We must remember that, at least for Christians, the cohabitation of rich and poor is a celebrated good in which God delights and upon which his Spirit rests. Jeremy Beer calls it "philanthrolocalism," the practice of charity understanding that charity's primary purpose, before even the alleviation of poverty, is simply "*authentic human communion.*"⁶ It is charity that first is proximity and intimacy. It's what the saints have always done; it's one of the chief reasons we recognize them as saints. Saint Francis of Assisi and Saint Teresa of Calcutta saw the poor and drew near to them. Frédéric Ozanam was a twenty-year-old law student when he and a few of his friends committed themselves to visiting the poor personally.⁷ Only then did the Society of Saint Vincent de Paul take shape. Beer quotes Maurin's friend Dorothy Day: "We should have hospices in all the poor parishes."⁸ Domingo de Soto, whom we encountered in the previous chapter, made the same argument. Seeing the poor, he insisted, was necessary for the cultivation of mercy. "In what way can a boy be instructed in that most sacred virtue without seeing or hearing the misfortunes of the poor with his own senses?" he asked. To remove the poor from our sight, he feared, would in time, morally

---

4. Francis, *Fratelli Tutti*, 76.
5. Maurin, *Easy Essays*, 26. See also Johnson, *Fear of Beggars*, 190.
6. Beer, *Philanthropic Revolution*, 99.
7. Misner, *Social Catholicism in Europe*, 59.
8. Misner, *Social Catholicism in Europe*, 92.

speaking, be disastrous. "Supposing these institutions that confine the poor remain in place for a century, those who are born now will never see beggars at the entrance of their house, nor will they go out to visit confined beggars. What feelings toward the poor could such people have?"[9] Removing the poor from our sight, de Soto worried we'd forget how to love the poor. Which arguably is what happened, for it is what's missing today in at least many affluent Christian communities and families—the moral formation that comes by way of seeing the poor. Sharing sacred spaces with the poor is what's absent from the daily lives of many churchgoers; and that is *the* problem, the idea we can practice our religion without the poor by our side.

But how to see again? Returning to the social scientists and journalists we followed briefly in the previous chapter, we discover the same moral instincts we find among the saints. For instance, about those who do the "dirty work" that sustains our clean and beautiful lives, Eyal Press asks, "What do we owe these workers?" He answers as well as any Christian should: "At minimum, it seems to me, we owe them the willingness to see them as our agents, doing work that is not disconnected from our own daily lives, and to listen to their stories, however unsettling what they tell us may be."[10] We must see that the lives of others, along with their work, are inextricably connected with ours. As the philosopher Alasdair MacIntyre puts it, we must prize not only the virtues of independence but also the "virtues of acknowledged dependence."[11] Because such virtues are necessary to being human. To be truly independent, truly rational, to contribute to the common good, is necessarily to flourish within a particular community, not formed by some reduced account of that community's virtues (think here of Pope Saint John Paul II's "economism," Pope Benedict XVI's "commercial logic," and Pope Francis's "consumerist individualism"[12]) but

9. Soto, *Deliberation on the Cause of the Poor*, 108.
10. Press, *Dirty Work*, 269.
11. MacIntyre, *Dependent Rational Animals*, 120.
12. John Paul II, *Laborem Exercens*, 13; Benedict XVI, *Caritas in Veritate*, 36; Francis, *Fratelli Tutti*, 222.

by an account of the virtues encompassing the whole of human flourishing and the genuinely common good. To illustrate his point, MacIntyre plays upon Adam Smith's famous image of the hypothetical, self-interested customer. MacIntyre imagines: "if, on entering the butcher's shop as an habitual customer I find him collapsing from a heart attack, and I merely remark 'Ah! Not in a position to sell me my meat today, I see,' and proceed immediately to his competitor's store to complete my purchase, I will have obviously and grossly damaged my *whole* relationship to him, including my economic relationship, although I will have done nothing contrary to the norms of the market."[13] Not to help, to act as if one has only a commercial relationship with the butcher, is obviously grotesque. And that's because, as MacIntyre continues, "Market relationships can only be sustained by being embedded in certain types of local nonmarket relationships, relationships of uncalculated giving and receiving, if they are to contribute to overall flourishing, rather than, as they so often in fact do, undermine and corrupt communal ties."[14]

But that is what has happened. Our communal ties have been corrupted within new global economies dominated by the likes of Amazon and Walmart. What are we to make, for instance, of the story Alec MacGillis tells of the deaths of Israel Espana Argote and Andrew Lindsey, two men killed when a tornado struck an Amazon sortation center in Baltimore in 2018? The day after they died, Amazon released a statement: "Due to the damage caused by Friday evening's severe weather, deliveries associated with this package sortation center are experiencing delays. We apologize for the inconvenience to our customers and are working quickly to resolve."[15] What virtues of independence exonerate we happily convenienced Amazon shoppers here? As one-click shoppers, what virtues of acknowledged dependence might we be lacking? In this new landscape of fulfillment centers, gig economies, and same-day delivery, what are the moral demands of our increasingly

13. MacIntyre, *Dependent Rational Animals*, 117.
14. MacIntyre, *Dependent Rational Animals*, 117.
15. MacGillis, *Fulfillment*, 290–94.

virtual economic ties? How do we see our neighbor? How might we continue to be moral in such a world?

We continue, MacIntyre says, by practicing the virtue of *misercordia*. Pope Francis similarly talks about *benevolentia*.[16] By these virtues we see others, particularly those in need of help, the vulnerable and hidden. Pope Francis points to the Good Samaritan who gives to the person in need of help the gift of his time and attention. In our fragmented age, he says, "our only course is to imitate the Good Samaritan."[17] Our morality is measured by our capacity to see others, especially the poor and the marginal. Over the years Catholics have described these virtues of acknowledged dependence in various ways. Anna Rowlands in her *Towards a Politics of Communion* helps navigate this terminology, particularly as it's found in papal teaching. From Pope John XXIII's talk of "socialization" to talk of "solidarity" in Pope Pius XII and Saint Pope John Paul II to talk of "charity" and "fraternity" in Pope Benedict XVI and Pope Francis, Catholic magisterial teaching has consistently asked us to think about our interdependence and the virtues such social reality demands.[18] Underneath these virtues is what we believe to be true of each human person. Seeing the human person in light of his or her origin and destiny—that is, that each person is created *imago Dei*, in the image of God, and that each person is capable of redemption in Christ—gives us a transcendent account of the value of each human being. This is what we mean when we talk about "human dignity," and it informs everything else. Creation, incarnation, redemption complete what we know about ourselves and in turn shape how we think about everything from economics, politics, and the environment to how we put up with in-laws. As *Gaudium et Spes* teaches, "all things on earth should be related to man as their center and crown."[19] To be moral is in every circumstance to acknowledge, protect, and serve

---

16. MacIntyre, *Dependent Rational Animals*, 125; Francis, *Fratelli Tutti*, 112.

17. Francis, *Fratelli Tutti*, 67.

18. Rowlands, *Towards a Politics of Communion*, 159, 240, 260–64.

19. *Gaudium et Spes*, 12.

each human person as a created and redeemed subject. It's to cherish each person's origin and end.

It is a vision of the human person bearing immediately upon how we think about work. If work is to be moral, it must be humane, for as Pope Leo XIII said, "with man it is different indeed."[20] Just as the state must not violate the dignity of citizens for the sake of some imagined greater good, the human person, *as worker*, must not be exploited by an employer for the sake of increased profits. An employer must not demand from workers that which degrades human dignity. Of course, Pope Leo XIII desired harmony between employees and employers, between the wealthy owner of capital and the worker, admittedly in an aristocratic and paternalistic sort of way. The worker must not "outrage the person of an employer"; likewise, the employer must "respect in every man his dignity as a man and as a Christian," he taught.[21] We are still a long way from Pope Francis's notion of "encounter" and the idea that even the poorest should be listened to and welcomed in dialogue.[22] But it's a start, and it's good to start somewhere. Because such basic mutual respect, that resists both violence and exploitation, also makes room for arguments for a just wage and the provision for other activities necessary to human flourishing, things like religion and leisure.

But as I said, for Pope Leo XIII, these were more defensive maneuvers than anything else. *Rerum Novarum* was trying to safeguard the humanity of both workers and employers and to keep peace. For a more developed theology of work—or at least, in papal teaching, the beginnings of one—we must turn to Pope Leo XIII's successors. For instance, in *Laborem Exercens* Pope Saint John Paul II begins with the traditional Christian claim that work is something rooted in creation. Humans worked before the fall because they were created to work, for it belongs to human nature to do so.[23] Thus, within human nature is a "mandate" to

---

20. Leo XIII, *Rerum Novarum*, 5.
21. Leo XIII, *Rerum Novarum*, 16.
22. Francis, *Fratelli Tutti*, 30.
23. John Paul II, *Laborem Exercens*, 1.

Discerning the Body and Seeing the Sabbath

"subdue, to dominate the earth." Humans were created to work in such a way that it "reflects the very action of the creator of the universe."[24] Our fall into sin did not change this basic truth of human nature; rather, it meant that, after the fall, work too was subject to redemption, a happy fault curiously elevating the purpose of work. Now redeemed in Christ, the human being, *as redeemed worker*, becomes a person whose work becomes Christ's work, "a living participation in his threefold mission as priest, prophet, and king."[25] Work becomes something through which Christ redeems the world; it becomes an extension of Christ's consecrating priestly rule. As Herbert McCabe long ago put it, our work becomes "not only a humanising of the world but an offering of the human thing to the Father."[26] Now part of Christ's redeeming work, our work shares in Christ's offering of a redeemed world to the Father (1 Cor 15:24). Work after the resurrection now shares in redemption. This is the theological context in which Pope Saint John Paul II talks about a "spirituality of work," which includes the practice of Sabbath rest. Humans not only have a natural "right to rest," rest is also a practice whereby we imitate God who rested on the seventh day.[27] But also, as Pope Saint John Paul II elaborates in his apostolic letter *Dies Domini*, fulfilled in Christ, the Sabbath becomes, as on the first Easter, a day that the disciples encounter the presence of the risen Lord and renew their life in him, carrying throughout the other days of the week the new creation within the old.

Here, however, more needs to be said. Seeing the poor or not seeing the poor, the reality or unreality of our religion, the theology and spirituality of work—all we've discussed so far—seem at this stage like puzzle pieces strewn about a table. How do they fit together? This is precisely where we need to think more about the Sabbath, for it's the missing piece needed to put it all together.

To help us do this let us turn for a moment from popes to a Protestant, particularly to the great Swiss theologian Karl Barth.

24. John Paul II, *Laborem Exercens*, 1.
25. John Paul II, *Laborem Exercens*, 24.
26. McCabe, "Theology and Work—A Thomist View," 220.
27. John Paul II, *Laborem Exercens*, 19, 25.

He can help us connect the dots. Barth's theology of the Sabbath has something to offer Catholic thought, looking at it from an angle slightly different from what we find in standard Catholic theologies rooted, as they are, in creation and the incarnation and in the anthropology and personalism that stem from those dogmas. How does he approach work and the Sabbath? Barth says it's important to think about the Sabbath *first*. Before we can understand what work is for, he argues, we must understand the Sabbath. Thus, he begins:

> What does the Sabbath commandment say? It speaks of a limiting of man's activity to the extent that this is, generally speaking, his own work, his own undertaking and achievement, the job he does for his livelihood and in the service of the community. It says that, in deference to God and to the heart and meaning of His work, there must be from time to time an interruption, a rest, a deliberate non-continuation, a temporal pause, to reflect on God and His work and to participate consciously in the salvation provided by Him and to be awaited from Him. It says that man's own work is to be performed as a work bounded by this continually recurring interruption. This interruption is the holy day.[28]

For Barth it is important that the Sabbath involves first a command to stop working. It is an *interruption* of work, "a clear delimiting and relativising of what man can and should will and do of himself."[29] The Sabbath is a sacrament of detachment. The purpose of the command, Barth says, is to forbid trust in one's own work. Sabbath rest cuts against the prideful delusions of self-will, teaching us slowly, by repeated observance, that God alone is omnipotent, the maker of all things, alone judge and savior. In this regard, the Sabbath prepares us to receive God's grace by ritually reminding us that we are *not* the Creator as we sometimes mistake ourselves to be. This is akin to what we read earlier, what Pope Benedict XVI said about Sunday in relation to sports, that Sunday

---

28. Barth, *Church Dogmatics* 3/4 §52, 46.
29. Barth, *Church Dogmatics* 3/4 §52, 49.

Discerning the Body and Seeing the Sabbath

reminds us that "our life is more a gift than an achievement."[30] It's also something close to Simone Weil's idea of "decreation."[31] Barth calls such faith formed by the Sabbath a "renouncing faith," for it "demands the faith in God which brings about the renunciation of man, his renunciation of himself, of all that he thinks and wills and effects and achieves."[32] Such faith resists the more egotistical aggressions of pride, ultimately a satanic impulse. Its fruit is a humility proper to creatures:

> He who has a self-renouncing faith on Sunday will have it also on a week-day. In the week he may and will work conscientiously and industriously, but neither as the lord nor as the slave of his work (just as on Sunday he is neither the lord nor the slave of his rest). He may and will do so with a good conscience, but aware that he cannot boast of it, that it cannot save him or defend him and that he can take comfort only in God. In the week he will have to fix his eyes on one aim after another, yet not fall under the domination of any material or spiritual, individual or collective Mammon. As he is busy on the everyday, he will also rest; as he fights on the everyday, he will also be at peace; as he works on the everyday, he will also pray. At the same time he will both grasp completely and let go completely.[33]

The Sabbath as "renouncing faith" slows us down, makes us creaturely again. Barth calls this the "humanitarian" good of the Sabbath. We may even call it a secular good.

In fact, one need not look hard to find such secular longing for the Sabbath. As Judith Shulevitz begins her book *The Sabbath World*: "At some point we all look for a Sabbath, whether or not that's what we call it."[34] In *The Day the World Stops Shopping*, as the title suggests, J. B. MacKinnon wonders what would happen if

---

30. Lixey et al., *Sport and Christianity*, 231.
31. Weil, *Gravity and Grace*, 78–86.
32. Barth, *Church Dogmatics* 3/4 §52, 55.
33. Barth, *Church Dogmatics* 3/4 §52, 67.
34. Shulevitz, *Sabbath World*, xiii.

Why Sunday Matters

one day the world suddenly stopped shopping. "What happens in the first hours and days of a world that stops shopping? How do we parse our wants and needs? Whose life changes the most and whose the least?" It's an urgent thought experiment given what our habits of consumption have done to the planet. "We must stop shopping but we can't stop shopping: the consumer dilemma has become, quite simply, the question of whether we can sustain human life on Earth," MacKinnon suggests.[35] Thinking from this environmental perspective, MacKinnon looks almost nostalgically to an earlier America governed by the blue laws which once prohibited most Sunday trade. Eliminating blue laws quickly changed us, MacKinnon says, and not for the better: *"people themselves were different on Sundays."*[36] One effect is that with the rise of the 24/7 economy, whatever collective "non-commercial" time we once enjoyed as a society is gone, resulting in a sort of "time famine," that particularly modern "feeling of unrelenting busyness." That's because with everything open all the time, we are never forced to rest collectively. Instead, we are conditioned to fill every free minute with activity, subjected to ubiquitous advertising inviting us to indulge in some kind of consumption, a conditioning, as we'll see in the next chapter, aided and abetted by technology. Under these circumstances even leisure becomes a commodity, a thing one may or may not be able to afford. And many no longer can. The working poor, for instance, are often robbed of leisure under just such a regime, now that stores (which must be staffed) are always open. Fallen under consumerist logic, many have been priced out of leisure.[37] It's also contributed, as we saw in the previous chapter, to an increase in consumption that is environmentally disastrous and clearly unsustainable. This is why MacKinnon longs for the return of something like blue laws. "Sunday closing sounds quaint to modern ears, but if it were implemented tomorrow, it would amount to an immediate 15 percent drop in shopping time."[38] He

---

35. MacKinnon, *Day the World Stops Shopping*, 12.
36. MacKinnon, *Day the World Stops Shopping*, 47.
37. MacKinnon, *Day the World Stops Shopping*, 48.
38. MacKinnon, *Day the World Stops Shopping*, 44.

Discerning the Body and Seeing the Sabbath

echoes Chief Justice Earl Warren's half-century-old secular defense of Sunday closings. Warren thought it clearly in the public interest to set aside a common day of rest—for *all*.[39] MacKinnon argues the same, that if rest is to serve the common good, it must be imposed upon all; it must be a shared social practice.[40] Blue laws don't just interrupt consumption, they encourage non-commercial behavior. MacKinnon points to Paramus, New Jersey, in Bergen County, one of the last places in America to prohibit most Sunday shopping. "In Paramus, the parking lots of eldercare homes have always been full on Sundays," MacKinnon notes.[41] "Six days a week, Bergen and especially Paramus, is a hypermodern bazaar of sales, trinkets, trends, fashions, distractions and technologies, all packed into the kinds of malls where your boot prints are quickly mopped up to sparkle behind you. One day a week, it stops." Speaking to longtime resident Paul Cotillo, MacKinnon asks if Paramus's blue law is an "act of anti-consumerism"? But that's not how he thinks of it. "We call it 'quality of life,'" Cotillo says.[42] MacKinnon longs for something like the Sabbath—for Barth's "renouncing faith"— because, as he realizes, it makes us a different kind of people, better for the earth and for each other.

Yet here Barth quickly insists that the Sabbath means more than this, that it rests upon more than "a humanitarian basis." "Man's Sunday refreshment, and therefore the fulfilling of this real need, the victory of this incontestable law, cannot be worth much if all it means is that man need not work on Sunday." Sounding like a worn-out parent, Barth even mentions "sporting events," among other weekend activities, that often fill a Sunday. "It is true that a holy day celebrated like this relieves man of none of the burdens but only lays new ones on him, that it entails no refreshment but only further toil."[43] Pope Saint John Paul II said the same, that

---

39. Laband and Heinbuch, *Blue Laws*, 48.
40. Laband and Heinbuch, *Blue Laws*, 49.
41. MacKinnon, *Day the World Stops Shopping*, 54.
42. MacKinnon, *Day the World Stops Shopping*, 45.
43. Barth, *Church Dogmatics* 3/4 §53, 57.

faith, not utility, gives the Lord's Day its "deeper meaning."[44] We should remember the "particularity" of the Sabbath, Barth says. The Sabbath is holy by decree of the God of Israel. It is a command given to the Jews, the observance of which week by week shapes a particular people—Israel. The primary purpose of the Sabbath therefore—which for Christians is also the primary purpose of the Lord's Day—is to gather the people of God for "divine service," to hear and to be shaped by the word of God, which in turn reveals Israel and the Church and makes it present.[45] For Christians, this is how we begin to understand the sacramentality of the Church. "The community assembled around the Gospel is the concrete Christian form of human fellowship," Barth says.[46] This is what happens through Sunday worship: the body of Christ takes visible form. Which is exactly what *Sacrosanctum Concilium* says, that "it is through the liturgy, especially, that the faithful are enabled to express in their lives and manifest to others the mystery of Christ and the real nature of the true Church." On the Lord's Day, in the liturgy of the word of God and the liturgy of the Eucharist, the Church renews its tangible, sacramental form as the body of Christ, "human and divine, visible but endowed with invisible realities."[47] The Sabbath, therefore, isn't merely about rest in humanitarian or secular terms but about rest given in the risen Christ. The Sabbath is about the liturgical and sacramental advent of Christ and that advent's effects. Signaled in the gift of the *pax*, given first liturgically after Christ is made sacramentally present on the altar and then ecclesially as priest, deacon, and people "offer each other the sign of peace," the rest which Christ inaugurates by means of the Church's peace demands a new ethics. More than mere rest, the Sabbath is about the beginning of a wholly different world.

Which helps us understand things like work. The purpose of Sunday is to express and manifest the Church, the body of Christ, in whose peace genuine rest is found; and so too, as we saw in

44. John Paul II, *Dies Domini*, 13.
45. Barth, *Church Dogmatics* 3/4 §52, 58–63.
46. Barth, *Church Dogmatics* 3/4 §52, 66.
47. *Sacrosanctum Concilium*, 2.

Discerning the Body and Seeing the Sabbath

Laborem Exercens, is it the Christian purpose of work.[48] Both liturgy and work make present the form of Christ; which, Barth quickly points out, is necessarily the form of the servant.[49] The liturgical gift of peace, met with the work of peace, both taking form as the body of Christ, a servant body, demands an ethics of solidarity which sees the union of God's people in union with God (what both the liturgical *pax* and the Sabbath ultimately signify) as the end of both work and worship.

The Sabbath teaches us we all belong. It's the mystery given in sacramental grace, in the Scripture and the Eucharist. This brings us back to the problem with which we began, that our worship has become unreal to the extent that we no longer see the poor, detestable to the extent we are no longer bothered by their absence. The Sabbath teaches us why exploiting the poor, why excluding them, is wicked. Because the poor are as much the people of God as anyone else, just a much the beneficiaries of God's *menuha* as the rest of us. In the Sabbath, which is Christ, the Church is renewed in this truth in word and sacrament, and by it we are trained to "discern the body," to see our brothers and sisters (1 Cor 11:29). Paul warned the Corinthians that their Eucharist was likely unreal because they did not celebrate it in solidarity (1 Cor 11:20). He begged them to "wait for one another" (1 Cor 11:33). This is what the Scripture teaches about the Sabbath, that it is this mystical, ethical gift. But this is precisely our problem. How many Christians think of Sunday in these terms? How many see Sunday Mass as anything more than a nagging "obligation" easily ignored? How many see Sunday biblically at all? Not many, I should think. So, then what can we do? The question I raised at the end of the last chapter remains: Is the Sabbath possible at all?

Yes, it is. The Sabbath is possible, and it's easier to realize than we may think. For it all begins locally—in homes, families, neighborhoods, and parishes. After mustering the courage to slow down, to stop, to live what Barth called a "renouncing faith," what we'll find, all within reach, are the simpler sources of happiness

---

48. John Paul II, *Laborem Exercens*, 24.
49. Barth, *Church Dogmatics* 3/4 §55–56, 148.

and holiness, a more human existence. For Pope Francis, writing near the end of *Laudato Si'*, it begins at Sunday Mass. There, he said, our eyes are opened:

> On Sunday, our participation in the Eucharist has special importance. Sunday, like the Jewish Sabbath, is meant to be a day which heals our relationships with God, with ourselves, with others and with the world. Sunday is the day of the Resurrection, the "first day" of the new creation, whose first fruits are the Lord's risen humanity, the pledge of the final transfiguration of all created reality. It also proclaims "man's eternal rest in God." In this way, Christian spirituality incorporates the value of relaxation and festivity. We tend to demean contemplative rest as something unproductive and unnecessary, but this is to do away with the very thing which is most important about work: its meaning. We are called to include in our work a dimension of receptivity and gratuity, which is quite different from mere inactivity. Rather, it is another way of working, which forms part of our very essence. It protects human action from becoming empty activism; it also prevents that unfettered greed and sense of isolation which make us seek personal gain to the detriment of all else. The law of weekly rest forbade work on the seventh day, "so that your ox and your donkey may have rest, and the son of your maidservant, and the stranger, may be refreshed" (Ex 23:12). Rest opens our eyes to the larger picture and gives us renewed sensitivity to the rights of others. And so the day of rest, centered on the Eucharist, sheds its light on the whole week, and motivates us to greater concern for nature and the poor.[50]

Sabbath rest is possible because somewhere close is a Christian community celebrating the Eucharist. There, in an imperfect parish church perhaps, Pope Francis suggests, individuals and families can find happiness and holiness, gifts of Christ's rest. It's not magic but simply the grace given to those who put themselves there—not once, not occasionally, but Sunday by Sunday. Pope Francis is talking about what can happen when Christians make Sunday Mass

---

50. Francis, *Laudato Si'* 237.

an ordinary feature of their lives. Eventually it will "open our eyes." We will see the poor and all else we need to see. We will see in time the beginning of the kingdom of God, what Jesus always talked about—the kingdom meant for us.

But what else can Christians do? Toward the end of *Dies Domini*, Pope Saint John Paul II made a simple suggestion. Why not, after Mass, practice solidarity? Instead of running off to the game or going back to work, maybe Christians can look, with their newly opened eyes, for those on the margins:

> If Sunday is a day of joy, Christians should declare by their actual behavior that we cannot be happy "on our own." They look around to find people who may need their help. It may be that in their neighborhood or among those they know are sick people, elderly people, children or immigrants, who precisely on Sundays feel more keenly their isolation, need and suffering. It is true that commitment to these people cannot be restricted to occasional Sunday gestures. But presuming a wider sense of commitment, why not make the Lord's Day a more intense time of sharing, encouraging all the inventiveness of which Christian charity is capable? Inviting to a meal people who are alone, visiting the sick, providing food for needy families, spending a few hours in voluntary work and acts of solidarity: These would certainly be ways of bringing into people's lives the love of Christ received at the eucharistic table.[51]

Earlier I suggested that maybe parishes could set aside occasional Sunday afternoons for casual play. Maybe they could also set aside an occasional Sunday to visit nursing homes, shelters, or the poor or lonely in the parish—anything that realizes the truth of the Eucharist beyond the walls of the church. By these simple acts of solidarity whatever is unreal or even detestable about our Sabbaths would begin to change. And that's because we would begin to change. For, changed slowly by sacrament and charity, we would become a bit more human, a bit more Christian.

---

51. John Paul II, *Dies Domini*, 72.

Why Sunday Matters

But what good will it do? If we're all implicated in an unjust world, in business models and supply chains and unsustainable, unethical habits of consumption, what effect will it have for one person, one family, one neighborhood, or one parish to practice the Sabbath in this way? Obviously, not much. But that's not the point. Banish from your mind the idea you need to save the world. Banish from your mind the idea you need to start a movement. Christians are not called to do anything like that. Rather, they are called to be faithful. Christians are called to live together as a sign of something different, the kingdom Jesus talked about. "To the Church falls the role of prophetic contradiction, and she must have the courage for that," Cardinal Ratzinger said, years before becoming Pope Benedict XVI.[52] Living the Christian Sabbath together as a prophetic sign is how we are to serve the broader mission of the Church. Whatever else needs to be accomplished, we may leave to God. Whatever course the world takes, Christians are called to remain faithful, no matter what little good we think it does for the world or however pointless it may at times seem. As the late John Hughes put it, "we remain under obligation to act rightly regardless of our chances of success, and, particularly according to the Christian logic of cross and resurrection, even if it comes at personal cost to ourselves. Holy working, trading, eating are in this sense a prophetic witness in the wilderness, ascetic and sacrificial."[53]

It's a course of Christian living that will indeed be numerically underwhelming. It will likely never become a movement. Here we again agree with the secular thinkers with whom we have journeyed. The Christian Sabbath is indeed a "minority ethic." MacKinnon is correct: "you can be the change you want to see in the world, but it will not change the world."[54] This is a way of life that in our day certainly belongs to the "fringes of the culture."[55] But that's the way we've long known it would be. Almost a century

---

52. Ratzinger and Seewald, *Salt of the Earth*, 241.
53. Hughes, *End of Work*, 230.
54. MacKinnon, *Day the World Stops Shopping*, 287.
55. Malesic, *End of Burnout*, 229.

ago Jacques Maritain spoke of a "new Christendom," a way of life—resistant to the false humanisms of modernity—that did indeed seek the "socio-temporal realization" of the Gospel.[56] That is, it's a way of life that is real, with tangible form, a distinct ethics, and a doctrine of political engagement. However, it is a Christendom born first in the "transfiguration" of the human person in grace, in the person *"changed* by grace."[57] Hence, Maritain said, this new Christendom will inevitably be small, "a sort of Christian diaspora, Christendom not grouped and united in a homogeneous body of civilization, but spread over the whole surface of the globe like a network of centers of Christian life disseminated among the nations."[58] The Christian Sabbath is indeed, to use Anna Rowlands's term, "a mystical-political practice," something akin to the practices of South American base communities.[59] It's a practice, in MacIntyre's terms, that belongs to those local forms of community he thought necessary to withstand the "new dark ages which are already upon us."[60] The Sabbath is not merely a bourgeois strategy for dealing with stress. It's something deeper, the mystical opening of a new creation. Which inaugurates a sort of seeing, as Saint Augustine imagined heaven might be, whereby we not only see God but see him in each other—a sort of seeing that's at once rest, love, and praise.[61]

56. Maritain, *Integral Humanism*, 155.
57. Maritain, *Integral Humanism*, 211.
58. Maritain, *Integral Humanism*, 312.
59. Rowlands, *Towards a Politics of Communion*, 274, 97.
60. MacIntyre, *After Virtue*, 263.
61. Augustine, *City of God* 22.29–30.

6

The Devil in the Garden

> Technology is now transforming the face of the earth...
> —*Gaudium et Spes*

THAT THE DEVIL HAD come wasn't the interesting bit. That demons had long harassed monks, and monks had long harassed demons, was simply the way of the desert. Supernatural bellicosity has always been, and remains, a reality of the desert. The devil is a regular there, especially in a desert filled with monks; seeing him wasn't news. Unlike an alien or a Sasquatch, seeing a demon was normal, entirely believable, not strange at all. In fact, it was expected.

Rather, what interested John Moschos, enough to write down the story Abba Irenaeus told him, is what the devil had done. The story is about one of the monks of Scêtê in northern Egypt who noticed one night the devil passing out gardening tools to the brethren. An odd thing, to be sure—again, not that he was there but what he was doing—the monk decided to ask the devil what he was on about. "What are these?" the monk asked. To which the devil replied, "I am presenting the brothers with a distraction to make them less assiduous in glorifying God." A simple answer, straightforward and spiritual, it's a story of devilish candor, an echo of Eden's temptation. Perhaps that is what Moschos found so interesting, that it offered a candid glimpse of the devil's normally hidden but unchanging motive, that he was still playing the same old game, offering evil under the appearance of good.[1]

It's also a story about technology, its ambiguity, and it sets the tone for our final meditation on the spiritual meaning and challenge of technology and on the relation between the Sabbath and the technologies we use and that sometimes use us. For the meaning of technology *is* spiritual. The challenges technologies offer are deeper than deciphering user manuals and troubleshooting. Technology demands spiritual discernment, not only because technologies can be both good and bad, but also because they shape us, change us, form our identities. Even things as benign as gardening tools: when used properly, they can help us cultivate the ground, grow food, and contribute to human flourishing; we can become farmers. But sometimes the devil hands out gardening tools. Implements designed to bring about growth can also distract and destroy. With the same tools in our hands we can lose perception of the sacred, lose sight of dignity, and become killers. Our technologies are beneficial and dangerous; they are always moral and spiritual. That's the warning implicit in the story about the devil and his gardening tools, that we should be spiritual enough to notice that sometimes it's the devil lending us a hand, to know when technology becomes temptation. Because the devil is still playing Eden's game.

But what is technology? Before going further, it's necessary to collect a few workable definitions from which we can conceive a clearer idea of what we mean whenever we talk about, praise, or curse technology. For by the term, we often invoke different, sometimes overlapping, notions. In one sense, by technology we mean devices, material things, and human artifacts like smartphones, hammers, cars, computers, thermostats. But we can also mean skills or activities or certain kinds of knowledge. This is to

---

1. Moschos, *Spiritual Meadow*, 55.

see technology instrumentally, as means to ends.[2] As the aggregation of devices, technology is often understood broadly to be the measure of human progress, of our rising above the precarious drudgery of primitive existence. From Francis Bacon to Ray Kurzweil, the printing press to singularity and transhumanist utopias, the story of technology is often told in naively Whiggish terms as a tale of glory after glory of enlightenment and liberation.[3] Here technology comes to mean more than devices, something more like a cultural force, a mentality or even an ideology. The philosopher Albert Borgmann called this a "substantive" view of technology.[4] In the world of new media, the world of screens and social media, similarly, technology creates what Fr. Antonio Spadaro calls an "ambience" or what Samuel James calls an "epistemological environment—a spiritual and intellectual habitat—that creates in its members particular ways of thinking, feeling, and believing."[5] Such substantive and intellectual views of technology can be negative, however. Here Jacques Ellul comes first to mind with his notion of "technique." For Ellul, distinct devices didn't matter as much as the rationalizing mentality (technique) behind such devices, that is, our compulsion for *"absolute efficiency... in every* field of human activity."[6] Ellul considered such a mentality intrinsically totalitarian, that as technology progressed and efficiency increased, human freedom decreased.[7] He called it a "milieu," and it was inescapable.[8] "Determinism" is the name given to this fear, the concern that technology follows its own logic, shaping users to its own ends instead of the other, more human, way around. We'll note similar fears below in the work of Ivan Illich, Wendell Berry, Brett Frischmann and Evan Selinger; in different ways each worried about what technology has taken away from

2. Coeckelbergh, *Introduction to Philosophy of Technology*, 5–6.
3. See, for example, Huttenlocher et al., *Age of AI*, 19.
4. Borgmann, *Technology and the Character of Contemporary Life*, 9.
5. Spadaro, *Cybertheology*, vii; James, *Digital Liturgies*, 9.
6. Ellul, *Technological Society*, xxv.
7. Ellul, *Technological Society*, 125.
8. Ellul, *Perspectives on Our Age*, 49.

us. One also thinks here of Lewis Mumford's "megamachine," by which he meant the rational ordering of human beings in the service of some perceived higher cosmic order—an order politically, religiously, and culturally enforced. An ancient technological reality, Mumford argued, as an example, he pointed to all the forces—hieratic, philosophical, scientific, and political—that organized innumerable ancient Egyptians sufficient to build the pyramids; that was the first megamachine—a human machine constructed from peasants and priests, soldiers and pharaohs.[9] An invisible machine, a totalizing technology comprising concepts, humans, and tools, he feared its return as technological progress, total war, the modern state, mass entertainment and propaganda, and the nuclear age came to define the twentieth century.[10] Technology for people like Ellul and Mumford meant more than any one device, or any aggregation of devices, but more a terrifyingly inescapable paradigm or frame, a relentless mentality. Returning to another of Mumford's notable examples, which we encountered earlier: a clock is a device, but the capitalist reordering of society the clock helped create is something else. Yet both relate to what we mean by technology. Not just another term for engineering, technology has always meant something more than devices, forced larger questions of meaning, and conjured myth.

Technology at times is itself myth. In the *Protagoras* Plato tells the story of Prometheus, how he "stole the wisdom of practicing the arts of Hephaestus and Athene, and fire with it." Humans were unable to protect themselves against nature; they were "naked and shoeless," and so Prometheus stole the technologies needed for human survival. It's a story mythologizing the instrumental aspect of technology. It's telling, too, that in this story we are also told what Prometheus did *not* steal (he didn't have time), and that is, "political wisdom." Zeus had to distribute that himself, and he knew he needed to, for without "justice and reverence" humans

---

9. Mumford, *Myth of the Machine: Technics and Human Development*, 188–94.

10. Mumford, *Myth of the Machine: The Pentagon of Power*, 257.

didn't stand a chance.[11] In the *Phaedrus* we find the story of an inventor named Theuth. Among other things, he invented writing; but, when he proudly presented his invention to King Thamus, the king was as much disturbed as he was impressed. For the technology of writing, he said, would not make humans wiser but instead forgetful. By itself writing wouldn't help anyone discover truth. One moral of this story is that the effects of technology are often unpredictable and beyond our control, "that to one man it is given to create the elements of an art, to another to judge the extent of harm and usefulness."[12] It's another ancient story about technology's ambiguity. These and other ancient stories are as ambivalent as any modern philosophy of technology, but they also agree on another point. And that is, our technologies are not just tools in our hands, rather, they are part of us; they become part of us. Technology, these stories suggest, belongs to human nature; we are *homo faber*. Watching the first fifteen minutes of Stanley Kubrick's *2001: A Space Odyssey*, for instance, we can't help but recognize ourselves. After the ape discovers he can make tools and weapons from bones, we understand that to be an evolutionary discovery, signaling that that primitive creature is on its way to becoming us. Because technology, our tools, are part of what makes us human. As Elon Musk said once, "The thing that people, I think, don't appreciate right now is that they are already a cyborg."[13] Perhaps that's one of the lessons these ancient stories teach: how long that's been true.

But this isn't just pagan wisdom. It's Jewish and Christian wisdom too. Technology is a "profoundly human reality," Pope Benedict XVI taught. He read the biblical story of creation as, among other things, a technology myth. Settled in the garden, man was "to cultivate and care for it" (Gen 2:15). "Technology enables us to exercise dominion over matter, to reduce risks, to save labour, to

---

11. Plato, *Protagoras* 321c–322d.

12. Plato, *Phaedrus* 274e–275. See also Coeckelbergh, *Introduction to Philosophy of Technology*, 15–16.

13. Frischmann and Selinger, *Re-Engineering Humanity*, 126.

improve our conditions of life," he taught.[14] Technology belongs to the prelapsarian ordering of creation. Related to work, technology also "bears a particular mark of man and of humanity."[15] This, as we'll see, an important point to make. Because to suggest (and this is the first theological thing to be said about technology) that the name of *homo faber* is Adam is to insist that sacred stories, the Scripture, faith, and theology do indeed bear upon how we think about technology. It's to insist, as Prometheus knew, that God still holds the wisdom necessary to put technology to good use and not evil, that technology can never rid itself of theology.

The ambiguities of technology are found throughout the Scripture. It is not farfetched to suggest that the whole of salvation history can be told as a story of God's technology saving us from ours. For instance, with human technology, to serve pride and stave off fear, the people of Shinar built the tower of Babel. "Come, let us build ourselves a city and a tower with its top to the sky, and so make a name for ourselves; otherwise we shall be scattered all over the world" (Gen 11:4). But also with human technology, this time with divine guidance, the people of God built and furnished the tabernacle, the tent of meeting where God spoke to Moses (Exod 26–27, 33:7–1; 35–38). By technology was wrought the golden calf of apostasy (Gen 32) but also the Siloam tunnel, a feat of engineering that not only stands to this day, but which was also a technology of resistance and life (2 Kgs 20:20; 2 Chr 32:30). As often as not, ordinary agricultural tools, or even bones, become weapons in the Bible. Samson killed a thousand men with the jawbone of an ass (Judg 15:15); Cain killed his brother with a bone too according to some legends. Jael used a tent peg to kill Sisera (Judg 5:21). The Bible is full of the technology of violence. But then, on the other hand, Christ turned the Roman technology of execution into a technology of salvation. The New Testament, in a sense, can be read as a story of technology's redemption, of the faithful being made God's "handiwork" and of the building of a kingdom by the peaceable technologies of preaching and sacraments that will be

14. Benedict XVI, *Caritas in Veritate*, 69.
15. John Paul II, *Laborem Exercens*, 1.

perfected ultimately in a heavenly Jerusalem measured out with golden tools (Eph 2:10; Rev 21:15).

Technology cuts both ways, even in the Bible—at least this side of the heavenly Jerusalem. As both Neil Postman (by no means a technology enthusiast) and Pope Saint John Paul II (notably positive from among numerous papal allies of technology) said, technology is "both friend and enemy."[16] Nuclear technology, for example, can be used either to heat homes or vaporize them. Social media can either inform and connect or misinform and divide. Belgian philosopher Mark Coeckelbergh calls this "dual use," and it is, as we've seen, what's always been true of technology—its ambiguity.[17] To deny the ambiguity of our technologies is to commit the "designer's fallacy."[18] Technology can always go one way or another or even another still. Again, think about Mumford's example of the clock. "The paradox, the surprise, and the wonder are that the clock was invented by men who wanted to devote themselves more rigorously to God; it ended as the technology of greatest use to men who wished to devote themselves to the accumulation of money," Postman observed.[19] The question therefore is what to do about the ambiguity of technology. What's the right response, fight or flight? Flight is an illusion. If technology existed in some form ever since Eden, it is silly to think one could ever be rid of it. Again, to quote Neil Postman, quoting the poet Stephen Vincent Benét, the best one can say is, "It is here."[20] Both overly negative and overly positive assessments of technology ultimately fail to offer workable guidance. Even for a technological pessimist such as Ellul, for whom technology "contains simultaneously the good *and* the bad," nostalgia is out of the question; "it has no survival value in the modern world and can only be considered a flight into dreamland."[21] But neither does Whiggish technological

---

16. Postman, *Technopoly*, xii; John Paul II, *Laborem Exercens*, 5.
17. Coeckelbergh, *Introduction to Philosophy of Technology*, 3.
18. Frischmann and Selinger, *Re-Engineering Humanity*, 45.
19. Postman, *Technopoly*, 15.
20. Postman, *Technopoly*, 39–40.
21. Ellul, "Technological Order," 91, 102.

optimism offer anything beyond the seductions of shallow consumerism; this too is a dreamland. As philosopher of technology Shannon Vallor puts it, "Naïve technophilia and reactionary technophobia are equally blind and unthinking responses to techno-social challenges."[22] But what should be our approach? We must "negotiate with technology," Postman said; the question is whether we will negotiate intelligently. We are in no different a spot from that nameless ancient monk with which we began our reflection. We are still wondering what our technologies do and mean.

Negotiating technology is an urgent and existential business because, as I said, technologies shape us. Technology "changes us and our thinking," Coeckelbergh insists; it is "*not* a mere instrument."[23] On this both techno-optimists and techno-pessimists agree; they disagree only about the extent and value of such change. But how to start? To assess such change, it is best to start with devices themselves, to begin not by thinking about technology in the abstract but, as Don Ihde put it, with "technologies in their particularities."[24] Brett Frischmann and Evan Selinger do this in their book *Re-Engineering Humanity*. Describing what they call "techno-social engineering," it is, they argue, one of the critical issues facing humans in the twenty-first century. Techno-social engineering happens when "technologies and social forces align and impact how we think, perceive, and act."[25] Take, for example, a technology such as GPS. Frischmann and Selinger, along with others, argue that by coming to rely on GPS we lose the ability to do things like navigate the world, or even our neighborhood. We lose the embodied knowledge and skills of stars and maps and instead become entirely dependent upon a technological device. Our agency is decreased, and we become "conditioned to obey" our devices, vulnerable in the absence of technology.[26] We suffer

---

22. Vallor, *Technology and the Virtues*, 219.
23. Coeckelbergh, *Introduction to Philosophy of Technology*, 6–7.
24. Coeckelbergh, *Introduction to Philosophy of Technology*, 53.
25. Frischmann and Selinger, *Re-Engineering Humanity*, 1–4.
26. Frischmann and Selinger, *Re-Engineering Humanity*, 6.

Why Sunday Matters

from "digital amnesia."[27] This is why, for instance, the United States Navy, after it stopped teaching sailors how to navigate by the stars, quickly reversed course. For what happens when technology fails or is hacked?[28] It's also the concern of some about artificial intelligence, that it "hastens the dynamics that erode human reason."[29] Modern technology has made us strangely powerful and vulnerable at once, comically dependent upon the devices we've come to need. The way Wendell Berry put it is that "most people now are living on the far side of a broken connection, and that this is potentially catastrophic. Most people are now fed, clothed, and sheltered from sources, in nature and in the work of other people, toward which they feel no gratitude and exercise no responsibility." To participate in today's technological economy, Berry said, "one must agree to be totally ignorant, totally passive, and totally dependent on distant supplies and self-interested suppliers."[30] Technological dependence also raises questions about who designs technologies and what their goals are. Who wields power in this brave new world? Frischmann and Selinger worry about the political and commercial nudges, the hidden curricula, choice framing, and engineered consent potentially embedded in the design of the technologies we depend upon. They fear these "technologies run the risk of turning humans into simple machines under the control or influence of those in control of the technologies."[31] They worry about who writes the code in a world increasingly dependent upon technology.[32]

Albert Borgmann's *Technology and the Character of Contemporary Life* also follows this phenomenological approach. He shows how technology is not only a deskilling force but one that also dismantles social relations. Borgmann's famous illustration is of the hearth, the fireplace or stove. Before the advent of central

27. Alter, *Irresistible*, 242.
28. Frischmann and Selinger, *Re-Engineering Humanity*, 100.
29. Huttenlocher et al., *Age of AI*, 207.
30. Berry, *Citizenship Papers*, 48, 74.
31. Frischmann and Selinger, *Re-Engineering Humanity*, 3, 82, 111.
32. Frischmann and Selinger, *Re-Engineering Humanity*, 262.

The Devil in the Garden

heating, warming a house took work; one had to build a fire. "And before it could be built, trees had to be felled, logs had to be sawed and split, the wood had to be hauled and stacked." It was work that often employed the entire family. "The mother built the fire, the children kept the firebox filled, and the father cut the firewood." Now, of course, a stove is technological too, but here Borgmann makes a distinction between a "thing" and a "device." A fireplace is a *thing* in that it is inseparable from its environment; a thing engages its environment differently than a device does. The fireplace, as a thing, "provided for the entire family a regular and bodily engagement with the rhythm of the season that was woven together of the threat of cold and the solace of warmth, the smell of the wood smoke, the exertion of sawing and carrying, the teaching of skills, and the fidelity of daily tasks." The "world of the fireplace" was a social world, but that's precisely what changed once the technological device of central heating was introduced.[33] Warmth, Borgmann argues, simply became a commodity to be purchased. The social cooperation, the work of a family, necessary to warm a home was no longer required. Heat is now simply purchased; the family is now simply a unit of consumers of the commodity of heat. This was also Ivan Illich's complaint about modern technological convenience, that it reduces people to "mere consumers." Illich thought that tools should be "convivial," that is, they should facilitate social cooperation rather than competitive consumption—the former, creating cultures; the latter, diluting cultures into a single bland monoculture.[34] The same happens with cooking. With the rise of fast food and other modern conveniences, the laborious tradition of cooking changes. Cooking is made easy, or sometimes entirely unnecessary, which may indeed be convenient, but it also eliminates the communal labor of preparing a meal.[35] "The practice of preparing a traditional meal, of setting the table, of saying grace, of conversing and eating thoughtfully is partly surrendered to the machinery of a fast-food chain and partly lost. The meal

33. Borgmann, *Technology and the Character of Contemporary Life*, 42.
34. Illich, *Tools of Conviviality*, 11.
35. Borgmann, *Technology and the Character of Contemporary Life*, 59.

has been impoverished to ordering and consuming standardized foods."[36] Food becomes something we mostly purchase instead of grow and prepare. We may watch professionals and hobbyists cook on television, but we rarely cook anything ourselves. The custom of the family meal is "shattered and disintegrates into snacks, T. V. dinners, bites that are grabbed to be eaten." "This is increasingly the normal condition of technological eating," Borgmann wrote forty years ago.[37] And the problem with this, Borgmann suggests, is that when a family is disburdened of such labor, that can lead to the disengagement of the family. Things that once ordered and shaped social engagement—what he called "focal practices"—are reduced to "shallow commodities, and our once profound and manifold engagement with the world is reduced to narrow points of contact in labor and consumption."[38] Which explains, Borgmann feared, "the growing emptiness of family life." "Since less and less of vital significance remains entrusted to the family, the parents have ceased to embody rightful authority and a tradition of competence, and correspondingly there is less and less legitimate reason to hold children to any kind of discipline."[39] In other words, the more technology relieves the family of its traditional work the more it is relieved of its purpose, and the more the family is rendered an accidental grouping of individual consumers with little else to do than to prop itself up with sentimentality and to buy each other things.

But then introduce new media, social and modern media, into the family, and the emptiness Borgmann worried about decades ago almost seems quaint. As psychologist Catherine Steiner-Adair puts it, "Technology, social media, and the digital age have converged on the American family, first transforming it and now threatening to replace the deepest and most vital human connections that children need to grow and thrive."[40] "The kids are not

36. Borgmann, *Technology and the Character of Contemporary Life*, 104.
37. Borgmann, *Technology and the Character of Contemporary Life*, 204.
38. Borgmann, *Technology and the Character of Contemporary Life*, 77.
39. Borgmann, *Technology and the Character of Contemporary Life*, 226.
40. Steiner-Adair, *Big Disconnect*, 18.

alright. Not completely," she argues.[41] "Our expanded ability to be technologically connected on screens to the world almost anytime, anyplace, is unquestionably pulling us away from making families primary in our children's lives and in grown-ups' lives," she says.[42] It is simultaneously a hyperconnected but deeply disconnected brave new world:

> Designed to serve us, please us, inform us, entertain us, and connect us, over time our digital devices have finally come to define us. We step in and out of our various roles throughout the day as coworkers, family, and friends. But with our phones in our pockets, our laptops handy, and our panoramic screens, game systems, and online lives just a click away, for many of us our relationship with technology is our single most consistent domain. It is our digital backdrop and theme music. In any given moment, with a buzz or a ping, our devices summon us and we are likely to respond, allowing ourselves to be pulled away from our immediate surroundings and anyone in them, into a waiting world of elsewhere and others. Whether we use it for work, shopping, or socializing, for communicating with our children or their teachers, for wonderful reasons or sometimes for meaningless and addictive stuff, the effect is the same: We turn our attention away from those present.[43]

"Psychologically we are indeed in new territory," she argues.[44] But, of course, each of us can sense this on our own—that addled feeling, the twitch of the push notification. It's the feeling with which Nicholas Carr begins his book *The Shallows*. "Whether I'm online or not, my mind now expects to take in information the way the Net distributes it: in a swiftly moving stream of particles." It's the feeling, the worry, that we have become "chronic scatterbrains."[45] And addicted scatterbrains, at that. As Adam Alter claims in his book

41. Steiner-Adair, *Big Disconnect*, 294.
42. Steiner-Adair, *Big Disconnect*, 29.
43. Steiner-Adair, *Big Disconnect*, 4.
44. Steiner-Adair, *Big Disconnect*, 22.
45. Carr, *Shallows*, 7.

Irresistible, the rise of ubiquitous technology, mobile technology especially, has undoubtedly given many of us behavioral addictions. "This shift to mobile devices is dangerous, because a device that travels with you is always a better vehicle for addiction." From 2008 to 2015, Alter says, the average time adults spend on their phones increased from eighteen minutes a day to two hours and forty-eight minutes a day. He claims that there are some 280 million smartphone addicts glued to their phones today.[46] Which, for all of us, portends potentially a psychological and social disaster. And that's because, among other things, the correlation between the overuse of mobile technology and a lack of empathy is strong; the claim, as Shannon Vallor observes, that people "raised on information technology and new media are increasingly deficient in empathetic concern and/or prone to pathological narcissism," is just too disturbing and tracks too closely to experience to be dismissed out of hand.[47] This is not to suggest that spending time online or on social media will inevitably make a person a narcissist. There are in fact many beautiful examples to the contrary of empathic human connections made possible by social media. Yet it is hard to dismiss Steiner-Adair's claim that unless face-to-face conversation is made primary in children's lives, they will indeed develop "a seriously disordered understanding of what it means truly to communicate."[48] Failing to make eye-contact, unable to sustain empathetic attention for any reasonable length of time, unable to respond compassionately to the suffering or pain of others, unable to resist cruelty: we recognize this not only in ourselves but in our children too.[49] It cannot be dismissed as merely the anecdotal fear of overly worried parents and old people. As Sherry Turkle put it, what we are experiencing today in our ubiquitously screened world is a "distinctive confusion." Unsure whether our

---

46. Alter, *Irresistible*, 28.
47. Vallor, *Technology and the Virtues*, 137.
48. Steiner-Adair, *Big Disconnect*, 62.
49. Gehart, "Screening Screen Time."

The Devil in the Garden

technology has drawn us closer together or driven us further apart, she calls it the feeling of being "alone together."[50]

But this unnerving feeling is only the half of it, and it's why our discussion must turn again to the spiritual. A century ago, Romano Guardini sensed a similar confusion. In his *Letters from Lake Como* he wrote, "A strange unreality is coming over human beings and things."[51] Like Borgmann, he worried about the cultural cost of central heating. "Everything that was achieved by human experience before an open fire is a thing of the past," he lamented.[52] For Guardini, however, what more profoundly illustrated the change wrought by technology was the transition from sailboat to steamer. A sailboat, he said, cooperates with nature. "The lines and proportions of the ship are still very closely related to the wind and waves." A steamer, on the other hand, "presses on through the sea regardless of wind and waves."[53] For Guardini, modern technology is not first a matter of social disengagement, as it is for Borgmann; rather, first it divorces human beings from nature. That was also Nikolai Berdyaev's view. For him, modern technology is a tragedy that "consists in the rebellion of creation against its Creator."[54] The willfulness of modern technology Berdyaev considered sinfully inorganic. Because not only do Christians value the passive, the weak and crucified, above the willful and efficient, above technique, modern technology also changes the way humans relate to the rest of creation.[55] "The actualism and titanism of technique is in direct opposition to a passive, vegetative, animal existence in the womb of the *Magna Mater*, it destroys the coziness and warmth of organic life clinging to the soil."[56] And this, he thought, is precisely the religious problem of technology, because it ushers us into an inorganic, overly rational, managed,

50. Turkle, *Alone Together*, 14.
51. Guardini, *Letters from Lake Como*, 20.
52. Guardini, *Letters from Lake Como*, 15.
53. Guardini, *Letters from Lake Como*, 12–13.
54. Berdyaev, *Bourgeois Mind*, 39.
55. Berdyaev, *Bourgeois Mind*, 34.
56. Berdyaev, *Bourgeois Mind*, 46.

totalitarian world. Divorced from creation, we are divorced from natural time and space, something he worried "may be fatal for religious and spiritual life." Berdyaev's concern for "the crazy speed of contemporary civilization" is eerily contemporary.[57] Mark Coeckelbergh, for example, shares these same concerns about the inhuman speed of technologically paced time:

> We do not have much time. We do not have much time left. We better hurry up. That is at least the message we get from the sciences, from technologies, from media. Our digital clocks and calendars tell us that we need to move on to the next calendar item. The next meeting. The next task. Time is up. Our day is short. We have to work and live fast. We have deadlines. If we do not deal with our emails now, new ones will be added fast and we will lose control. If I do not plan a leisure event or take a course now, we will miss it. If we do not call our friend or our doctor now, it will be too late. If we do not buy this product, we miss out on something. We live in a society of acceleration and speed.[58]

Coeckelbergh fears that technologically paced time changes our experience of time, forcing us into a "presentism" wherein we forget the past and refuse to think realistically of the future, suffering a kind of ignorant short-termism.[59] Others have long worried about the same thing. Decades ago, Marshall McLuhan suggested that "perhaps man was not intended to live at the speed of light."[60] Adam Alter worries that since so little in our world happens slowly, "our brains respond more feverishly."[61] We experience this also as what Postman called the "annihilation of space."[62] This is Marshall

---

57. Berdyaev, *Bourgeois Mind*, 56.

58. Coeckelbergh, *Digital Technologies, Temporality, and the Politics of Co-Existence*, 2.

59. Coeckelbergh, *Digital Technologies, Temporality, and the Politics of Co-Existence*, 6.

60. Ripatrazone, *Digital Communion*, 97.

61. Alter, *Irresistible*, 44.

62. Postman, *Technopoly*, 68.

McLuhan's "global village," a not entirely benign image.[63] Stefan Zweig in his memoir, *The World of Yesterday*, at the very beginning of the world McLuhan later described, was deeply troubled by this. He didn't want to be present to the whole world all at once, but the radio he owned, the radios he heard walking the streets, wouldn't give him a choice. "Incidents thousands of miles away . . . came vividly before our eyes. There was no shelter, no safety from constant awareness and involvement. There was no country to which you could escape, no way you could buy peace and quiet," he wrote.[64] We know this feeling, this rush, the inescapability of it. Yet for Berdyaev the consequences were more than social and emotional. The effects of modern technology are more than psychological; it has more to do than with brain development and mental health. Rather, the threat of modern technology finally is that by divorcing human beings from the natural experience of time, it divorces them from the experience of genuine eternity, which is also to be divorced from any experience of God:

> Such a conquest of time through speed becomes an enslavement to the current of time, which means that in this relation technical activity is destructive of eternity. Man has no real time for it, since what is demanded of him is the quickest passage to the succeeding instant. This does not mean that we must see in the past the eternal which is being destroyed by the future: the past does not belong to eternity any more than does the future—both are in time. In the past, as in the future and at all times, an exit into eternity, the self-sufficient complete instant, is always possible. Time obeys the speed-machine, but is not mastered and conquered by it, and man is faced by the question: Will he remain capable of experiencing moments of pure contemplation, of eternity, truth, beauty, God?[65]

---

63. Ripatrazone, *Digital Communion*, 27.
64. Zweig, *World of Yesterday*, xv.
65. Berdyaev, *Bourgeois Mind*, 57.

In the speed of technology, we are torn from creation and contemplation is lost; the violence is both natural and spiritual. Remember what the devil said to that old monk, how he explained himself: "I am presenting the brothers with a distraction to make them less assiduous in glorifying God." Berdyaev shows us why that's a problem for more than piety and devotion. It's about what we are and what we may become. "The machine demands that man assume its image; but man, created to the image and likeness of God, cannot become such an image, for to do so would be equivalent to his extermination."[66] His fear was that, ushered into the rush of technological time "the last men will become like machines, then they will vanish."[67] Gabriel Marcel used the word "degradation" to name this technological deformation of human beings. "In our contemporary world it may be said that the more a man becomes dependent on the gadgets whose smooth functioning assures him a tolerable life at the material level, the more estranged he becomes from an awareness of his inner reality."[68] That is, like Berdyaev, Marcel feared that human beings rushed into a constantly endless feeling of *now* will lose the taste for speculative knowledge and the slow, passive gentleness needed to receive it. Which soon, he worried, "shuts out the very possibility of contemplation," eventually replacing philosophy with "misosophy," the love of wisdom with the hatred of wisdom.[69] Here we are at the very bottom of what we feel, the root of our anxiety about this technologically impressive world, an existential fear that there is something about it that is deleting us. This, more than Whiggish hubris, explains the various gnostic utopias of transhumanism and posthumanism, the fantasies of brain emulation, mind uploading, and artificial general intelligence. These are technologies clearly bearing "immortal longings," technologies that ironically want what they helped occlude.[70] But they, of course, are longings more

---

66. Berdyaev, *Bourgeois Mind*, 40.
67. Berdyaev, *Bourgeois Mind*, 55.
68. Marcel, *Man against Mass Society*, 41.
69. Marcel, *Man against Mass Society*, 48.
70. Shakespeare, *Antony and Cleopatra*, act 5, scene 2.

The Devil in the Garden

anxious, more virtual and unreal than our more primitive religious yearnings. They lead only to servers.

Which brings us finally to the Sabbath, what we'll search for in the next chapter. More than youth sports, more than our work, the danger of modern technology is that it does more than take time, it erases time. Youth sports or capitalism may seek to destroy the Sabbath or sin against it; modern technology seeks to delete it. Again, Berdyaev sensed what that means. "We are faced by the task of saving the very image of man," he said. "He has been called to continue creation and his work represents the eighth day: he was called to be king and master of the earth, yet the work he is doing and to which he was called enslaves him and defaces his image."[71] That's the danger of modern technology, the danger of that phone in your pocket, the tablet your child brought home from school: it demands an adoration so complete and constant that we not only lose God, we lose ourselves too. Which, thinking again of our modern Sunday Christ, if we were to portray this sin, such is how it would look: as the fading figure of a man, a woman, or a child, eyes glazed and glued to a screen, turned away from Crucified, both fading, distracted the one and unloved and forgotten the other. Spiritual deletion. Which is why we need holy time, a Sabbath, to remember God, our created selves too—to not be deleted, but to remain human.

---

71. Berdyaev, *Bourgeois Mind*, 59.

7

Digital Temporality and the Sabbath

It rests with man's spirit to escape this fate.
—Nicholas Berdyaev

Marshall McLuhan kept his television in the basement. "I did not want it invading my home," he said.[1] The great philosopher of new media worried what it would do to him. Not unlike that Egyptian monk who wondered what the devil was doing, McLuhan was at times strangely cautious about the technology and media we live with today without any thought. "Turn on, tune in, drop out," he is alleged to have said, but he certainly didn't want to do that himself, at least not in his own house.[2] His media consumption we would today consider strange, even paranoid. Maybe it wasn't paranoid at all, but wise. Whatever it was, it probably had something to do with his Catholicism, with his capacity to see things spiritually, to discern and not just troubleshoot.

1. Ripatrazone, *Digital Communion*, 98.
2. Ripatrazone, *Digital Communion*, xvi.

Digital Temporality and the Sabbath

In fact, he said as much. It was his faith, he claimed, that gave him an "emotional and spiritual economy denied to the confused secular mind."[3] It was his willingness to remain spiritual in an increasingly technological world that gave him his bearings. An ancient instinct, Prometheus, remember, stole the "arts of Hephaestus and Athene" but not political wisdom, the wisdom of "justice and reverence"; that remained with Zeus. McLuhan understood that, and so did that ancient monk. And it was, I think, Plato's point, that to wield well and wisely our technologies, whatever they are and however advanced they may be, we must still petition the gods, still seek the divine.

Pope Benedict XVI insisted that no matter how fascinating our technologies become, we remain morally responsible for them.[4] No matter how much our technologies progress, we must still seek moral wisdom, think morally, become moral people. It will always be necessary, whatever the disturbing wonders of artificial intelligence or the increased utility of our devices, to seek the knowledge Prometheus did not steal. For such knowledge can't be stolen but only prayed for and received freely. Yet this is not immediately a religious search; or better said, it is not necessary one immediately accept that it's religious or spiritual at all. To follow the philosophers, the writers, and even some engineers who've thought about this deeply is to go with them on a quest for this wisdom, on a winding and fractured and fruitful pilgrimage. It is to see through a mirror darkly (1 Cor 13:12). But it is genuinely to begin to see.

It is first an appeal, as Frischmann and Selinger call it, for a "new form of humanism."[5] Again, such appeals have been made for millennia. More recently, decades ago, Ivan Illich called for what he named "counterfoil research," by which be meant, in his technophobic manner, the capacity to detect "the incipient stages of murderous logic in a tool; and to devise tools and tool systems

---

3. Ripatrazone, *Digital Communion*, 10.
4. Benedict XVI, *Caritas in Veritate*, 70.
5. Frischmann and Selinger, *Re-Engineering Humanity*, 271.

that optimize the balance of life."[6] Our technologies should be utilized, and limited when necessary, he said, according to a vision of "convivial society" and not according to what is merely technologically possible or economically profitable. Frischmann and Selinger's idea of what this would look like is humbler and more realistic than Illich's return to convivial society, which he admitted would be painful.[7] At least to begin, Frischmann and Selinger suggest, such humanism would protect a person's "freedom to be off," to disconnect, to be forgotten online, to refuse digital immortality. It would also look like freedom from "engineered determinism," that is from various forms of techno-social engineering—choice framing, indecipherable electronic contracts, and the manipulation and planned obsolescence of "smart" household devices.[8] For Adam Alter it would look like rethinking the way our technological devices are designed. Doing away with modern technologies on the scale Illich thought necessary is neither desirable or possible; but neither, Alter insists, is it fate that our devices are designed the way they are. "It is possible to create a product or experience that is indispensable but not addictive," he argues.[9] But to do that we would have to question our economics and our politics, ask bigger questions. Which is Illich's salvageable point, Frischmann and Selinger's and Alter's point too—again, it was Plato's point—that some kind of transcendent wisdom is necessary, that without it technology does indeed become a deterministic nightmare, completely inhuman.

But this is not simply an appeal to carve out space in our increasingly technological world for things like religion or spirituality or the humanities, that we remember to begin and end in prayer, talk about "values," or that we make engineering students read Shakespeare—no matter how good those things are. Heidi Campbell and Stephen Gardner, for example, outline a fourfold process of engagement religious groups can follow to guide their

6. Illich, *Tools for Conviviality*, 77.
7. Illich, *Tools for Conviviality*, 14.
8. Frischmann and Selinger, *Re-Engineering Humanity*, 13.
9. Alter, *Irresistible*, 319.

use of technology. Understanding one's history, one's core beliefs, they rightly argue, enables religious groups to negotiate and continue to discern their engagement with various technologies.[10] This certainly is good as far as it goes, but there is much more to it than that. And that is, it is important to grasp that the wisdom necessary to keep technology human is embodied within material culture itself, not merely added later. That is, it is more than a question about how we use technology but also about how technology uses us. This is why Albert Borgmann's notion of focal practices remains essential to thinking well about modern technology. Focal practices, remember, are those common social acts or things that require social engagement or cooperation. Rituals or even places like cathedrals or town squares can constitute focal practices. Focal practices are often ordinary. Borgmann's famous example, which we've looked at already, is the practice of heating a home. In times past it took the work of the entire family to keep the fire of the hearth going. Now, however, as the hearth's task has been replaced by the technology of central heating, such social cooperation is no longer necessary. No longer the builders of fire, we've become the buyers of fire, needing now only to pay the electricity bill. Technology has rendered such social cooperation obsolete; now we need only worry about remaining solvent consumers. This is precisely the sort of change, repeated in innumerable instances, that Borgmann says we should notice, the loss of so many of our primeval focal practices. Because from the social cooperation born of focal practices are also born much of the wisdom we find in religion, spirituality, and the humanities; and by them is such wisdom sustained and handed down. Material culture is culture; and so, given the radical technological changes of recent centuries, radical cultural change was inevitable. Hence the need to rediscover or find or forge new focal practices.[11] Because human culture depends upon it.

Within our liberal order, however, that's difficult. And that's because the promises of technology and the guarantees of political

---

10. Campbell and Garner, *Networked Theology*, 103–4.
11. Borgmann, *Technology and the Character of Contemporary Life*, 245.

liberalism have canceled each other out. The promise of technology, since at least Bacon, has been to liberate us from the burdens of work and the cruelties of nature to pursue happiness unhindered. But the liberal tradition has rendered happiness a private matter. Thus, to renew focal practices on a scale that would socially engage the whole of society is no longer possible. There is no longer any hegemonic material culture, no truly hegemonic culture of any kind; thus, any new focal practice oriented toward a particular notion of happiness is bound to be smaller than in the past because particular conceptions of happiness will always be widely disputed.[12] Thus focal practices within technological society will be small, "humble and scattered," having suffered what amounts to a Rawlsian chastening.[13] Borgmann simply accepts this as fact, which is partly why he discounts the suggestion that something like the Eucharist could ever serve as a focal practice in the way it did centuries ago.[14] Instead, Borgmann looks to nature or running or other much smaller practices.[15] He does, however, argue that we must rethink political discourse, finding a way to accept and support various focal practices, even religious practices.[16] Elsewhere he talks about "communities of celebration," communities, including religious ones, that pursue focal practices that benefit wider liberal society and which should therefore even receive public support.[17] But by now our discussion has become no longer one about technology but about social theory and politics. But that's also the point. Prometheus didn't steal this wisdom; humans remain in need of it. And Borgmann reminds us that such wisdom is not merely some add-on spirituality easily gained, but that it remains thoroughly practical and concrete, something nearer the ancient notion of *pietas*.

12. Borgmann, *Technology and the Character of Contemporary Life*, 85–101.

13. Borgmann, *Technology and the Character of Contemporary Life*, 210.

14. Borgmann, *Technology and the Character of Contemporary Life*, 207.

15. Borgmann, *Technology and the Character of Contemporary Life*, 195, 200.

16. Borgmann, *Technology and the Character of Contemporary Life*, 232.

17. Borgmann, *Power Failure*, 54.

Digital Temporality and the Sabbath

Yet Borgmann's call for new focal practices, however necessary, Shannon Vallor nonetheless considers "ambiguous and incomplete."[18] Also necessary is an account of the virtues that is scaled globally and adapted to a world of rapid technological change—"technomoral virtues," she calls them. Grasping the ethical implications of modern technology is not easy, for we suffer from what Vallor calls "technosocial opacity."[19] That is, given the magnitude and speed of technological progress, where we are headed or what exactly are the consequences of technological changes remain opaque. Thus, Vallor draws her account of technomoral virtues from Aristotelian virtue ethics and Confucianism to offer "the philosophical equivalent of a blind man's cane."[20] What do honesty, self-control, empathy, civility, and magnanimity and so on look like in a technological world and in the world of new media? These are the enduring questions of moral habit that remain no matter the extent of technological progress, which in fact become more urgent. That's Vallor's contribution. Merely finding new focal practices or to insist upon less addictive or manipulative design is not sufficient. What is necessary, if we are not to be overrun by our technology, is to seek genuine "technomoral wisdom," which requires a coherent account of the virtues as well as "*collective* cultural agreement" and even the creation of "new institutions, communities, and cultural alliances."[21] Yet this is where Vallor's work is itself ambiguous and incomplete, for it is by no means clear whether her global vision for technomoral virtues would ever be either possible or even advisable. Nor, if Borgmann is correct about the cultural significance of focal practices, is it clear how one reconstructs an account of the virtues within the context of cultural devastation, especially on a global scale. Vallor herself clearly understands the dilemma; that's how she interprets the several utopianisms of transhumanists and other technosolutionists. The problem, she admits, is "who among us has the

---

18. Vallor, *Technology and the Virtues*, 30.
19. Vallor, *Technology and the Virtues*, 6.
20. Vallor, *Technology and the Virtues*, 10.
21. Vallor, *Technology and the Virtues*, 169, 248.

courage and genuinely magnanimous moral leadership to point the way to a positive vision of the human future?"[22] Yet it's a question she doesn't answer.

It is not hard to guess where I'm going with this. What may not immediately be a religious search does nonetheless become religious. Catherine Steiner-Adair, putting it in personal terms, yet still in vaguely marketable terms, gets a little closer when she argues that to flourish within the world of new media one should be open to "spirituality and the search for big meaning."[23] This is true. However, given the existential stakes of all we've said about technology, that it at times raises fundamental question even about humanity itself, we must say more, even if it's religious. That's why technological pessimists like Jacques Ellul remain valuably troublesome prophets, because they remind us of what succeeding generations of technocrats and engineers seem often eager to forget. And that is, that the "further technical progress advances, the more the social problem of mastering this progress becomes one of an ethical and spiritual kind." Ellul unapologetically insisted that our use of technology, even technology itself, must submit to the spiritual.[24] Otherwise, technology will itself take on the pretensions of the sacred and become exactly the frighteningly inhuman determinism people either fear or ignore. As Berdyaev warned, technology will replace the image of God with the "image and likeness of the machine" unless human beings remember what they are.[25] The issue is not only anthropological but also religious and ultimately theological. It certainly involves more than scheduling time for mindfulness. Lewis Mumford makes this point. Again, think of the opening sequence of Kubrick's *2001: A Space Odyssey*. Mumford's criticism of it likely would be that what it gets wrong is that it is not the tool which makes the primitive creature human. Birds with their nests and beavers with their dams are just as technologically impressive. Other animals use tools. Instead, it's

22. Vallor, *Technology and the Virtues*, 241.
23. Steiner-Adair, *Big Disconnect*, 291.
24. Ellul, "Technological Order," 95–96.
25. Berdyaev, *Bourgeois Mind*, 60.

Digital Temporality and the Sabbath

language and ritual and play that distinguish humans from other animals.[26] As Aristotle put it, human beings have *logos*.[27] If not always apparent or perfectly rational, we are at least always language animals; we are *homo symbolicus* and in time *homo religiosus*.[28] That is what human beings are. We are *imago Dei*, made in God's image and likeness, created *capax Dei*, open to the Creator. Thus, before the simplest tool was forged, before all crafts and engineering, what even begets the hoped-for digital eternities of artificial intelligence: before all that are those "immortal longings" uniquely and ineluctably human. Here we understand all the hidden Edens of science fiction—Mr. Charrington's room above the shop in Orwell's *1984*, the "Ancient House" in Zamyatin's *We*, and Huxley's New Mexico in *Brave New World*. All of it speaks to our inability to escape or technologically replace our created yearning. It's why Samuel James is correct, that "every time we log on, we are looking for something. We are looking for heaven."[29] Because even before Google, we have always been searching.

However, it is not enough merely to remember this fact. As we conceive, design, and use technology it is necessary but not sufficient that we remember what humans are. It is, of course, always sensible, even if sometimes seemingly rare, to think of users before design, but that's not the only question theology and ordinary believers should ask about technology. Rather, the question that follows is: If we human beings are made in the image of God, if the human creature is *capax Dei*, then how in concrete terms do we relate to God in our technological world? That is, after stating the anthropological and theological fact, what next? How do we resist the image of the machine? More than virtue ethics, more than focal practices and better design, the answer involves re-thinking time, or better, re-experiencing time.

Mark Coeckelbergh comes close to the answer in his discussion of digital technologies and temporality. His concern, as we

26. Mumford, "Technics and the Nature of Man," 78–79.
27. Aristotle, *Politics* 1253a10.
28. Taylor, *Language Animal*, 338.
29. James, *Digital Liturgies*, 181.

Why Sunday Matters

noted in the previous chapter, is that we suffer from "presentism," that, conditioned by our technologies to focus almost exclusively on the present, we are unrooted from the past while also being irresponsibly distracted from the future. Which makes presentism in fact a kind of "non-present," unmoored from reality and "emotionally burdensome."[30] Such is the effect of living in a world of multiple digital temporalities—the ceaseless affront of email, push notifications, endless news cycles. It is, Coeckelbergh contends, a true experience of a "change of time," the experience of "duration" in Bergsonian terms, which is an idea quite at home in disciplines like the philosophy of cinema.[31] Berdyaev, remember, made this same point but added that such temporal conditioning was not just inhuman but also "fatal for religious and spiritual life."[32] However, for Coeckelbergh, the first challenge is "to re-connect time to life and the lifeworld."[33] But how is that achievable? Coeckelbergh points out that the various digital temporalities we experience also have narrative structure; that is, to put it simply, each temporality has its own story. For example, there is my story and your story, each with its own temporal experience. But then there are cultural stories, national stories, geological stories; these too are experienced as different temporalities.[34] Digital technologies capture users within their own stories too, each experienced as time—often rushed. Which is precisely the concern: digital temporality is often an experience of time that is so fast, so instantaneous, that "presentism" is the result. We are forced to put on "technoperformances of time" that are ultimately inhuman—always present, always connected, always ready to reply, to post, to like, to comment. Thus,

---

30. Coeckelbergh, *Digital Technologies, Temporality, and the Politics of Co-Existence*, 6–9.

31. Coeckelbergh, *Digital Technologies, Temporality, and the Politics of Co-Existence*, 23. See, for example, Deleuze, *Cinema*.

32. Berdyaev, *Bourgeois Mind*, 56.

33. Coeckelbergh, *Digital Technologies, Temporality, and the Politics of Co-Existence*, 12.

34. Coeckelbergh, *Digital Technologies, Temporality, and the Politics of Co-Existence*, 30–31.

Digital Temporality and the Sabbath

to rescue ourselves from such presentism, we must discover other narratives, other experiences of time, and other ways to perform:

> If we do not like how our performances are governed and structured, by others and by technology, we have to actively make time in a different way. We have to actively resist how our time is governed, directed, and choreographed. Technologies and media, in the form of techno-performances in which we participate, render this more difficult as they pre-structure our time and thus shape our temporality and daily existence.[35]

We must practice new "synchronicities of resistance," Coeckelbergh argues, new experiences of time not ruled by either the economic, political, or technological order.[36] But to be successful, it must also be a recovery of "common time."[37] Going it alone, no one would be able—at least sanely—to experience time sufficient to resist the temporalities of the world. Coeckelbergh insists such a subversive project must be collective, for the further privatization of time only makes the problem worse.[38] To be strong enough to resist the presentist temporalities of our contemporary world, such a project of resistance must involve new narratives and institutions, new rituals; it must be a project that works "to establish an 'us.'"[39] This is why Coeckelbergh believes such a project is a political one, a matter of what he calls "kairopolitics."[40] Which, of course, is not wrong; but neither is it immediately correct. Here is where, as with the others we've discussed, Coeckelbergh fails

---

35. Coeckelbergh, *Digital Technologies, Temporality, and the Politics of Co-Existence*, 41.

36. Coeckelbergh, *Digital Technologies, Temporality, and the Politics of Co-Existence*, 68, 80.

37. Coeckelbergh, *Digital Technologies, Temporality, and the Politics of Co-Existence*, 63.

38. Coeckelbergh, *Digital Technologies, Temporality, and the Politics of Co-Existence*, 75.

39. Coeckelbergh, *Digital Technologies, Temporality, and the Politics of Co-Existence*, 81.

40. Coeckelbergh, *Digital Technologies, Temporality, and the Politics of Co-Existence*, 77.

Why Sunday Matters

to offer anything genuinely concrete, not beyond appeals for "forms of local and global non-capitalist, non-nationalist, and non-totalitarian synchronicity" that are still democratic but also strong enough to engage climate change and other global crises. But in practical terms what would that look like? We "cannot and should not romantically go back in time," Coeckelbergh insists.[41] True, but couldn't we recover at least some things from the past? Couldn't going back in time help maybe a little? Might there have been "synchronicities of resistance" in the past that would help us remain human in the present and into the future? Coeckelbergh doesn't seem open to such a possibility.

The problem with Coeckelbergh's otherwise excellent assessment is that the issue is not first political. And that's because our technologies challenge us at a deeper level, which is something both the warnings of techno-pessimists and the utopias of techno-optimists make clear. Rather—and although the problem is certainly one of time—it is first at once a problem that is anthropological and theological. Which is to say it is thus also at once religious, liturgical, and mystical. Time is not immediately an issue of politics. But here we come again to what for some is an embarrassing point, which many assume is better politely deflected; and that is, the matter is inescapably spiritual. Technologies in hand, we must still petition the gods—the true God in fact—receiving, if we are to remain human, the wisdom the true God gives, what he gave at the primeval beginnings of things and what he first called holy—sacred time set apart, the Sabbath. The original synchronicity of resistance, Abraham Joshua Heschel called the Sabbath "a palace in time."[42] Barth, remember, called it an "interruption."[43] Mumford called it a "curb" against the megamachine born of the need to hold on to the "inner life."[44] He argued we needed such

---

41. Coeckelbergh, *Digital Technologies, Temporality, and the Politics of Co-Existence*, 82.

42. Heschel, *Sabbath*, 15.

43. Barth, *Church Dogmatics* 3/4, §52, 46.

44. Mumford, *Myth of the Machine: Technics and Human Development*, 232.

curbs again: "individual minds, small groups, and local communities nibbling at the edges of the power structure by breaking routines and defying regulations." This, at the least, is why I wouldn't so quickly dismiss the rediscovery of the Sabbath as some romantic escape into the past.

But this again is not merely to defend an enclave of the spiritual within the immanent frame of the technological. It is not simply to hold one's own as a "loving resistance fighter," which is all Neil Postman can say.[45] It is instead to recover our capacity for contemplation, what Berdyaev said we had lost, having become slaves of the machine's "now."[46] It is to make "an act of faith," as Marcel put it, to stand not before the technological "world of the problematic" but before the "world of mystery."[47] The Sabbath opens wide the door of contemplation. And the door is liturgy. This is why the Sabbath is necessary and why the mere practice of mindfulness is not sufficient to withstand the dehumanizing strength of digital temporalities. Only the Mass, to follow the philosopher Catherine Pickstock, is able to transgress such "mundane chronologies," offering the only truly "redemptive critique of secular time."[48] And that's because by joining in the angelic liturgies ("And so, with Angels and Archangels . . . ") and by speaking in the voice of the Son ("TAKE THIS, ALL OF YOU, AND EAT OF IT . . . ")—with stammering voice and angelic apostrophe—we enter into "dislocationary time," and "uncovered time."[49] And we find ourselves in an unstable, indeterminate place (for, what is it, where is it, to begin "*In* the name of the Father, and of the Son, and of the Holy Spirit"?) made liturgical pilgrims and beggars, humbled and opened by the liturgy's ceaseless repetition.[50] Impersonating these angelic divine voices, the liturgical beggar "cannot but participate

---

45. Postman, *Technopoly*, 182.
46. Berdyaev, *Bourgeois Mind*, 57.
47. Marcel, *Man against Mass Society*, 66–67.
48. Pickstock, *After Writing*, 221–23.
49. Pickstock, *After Writing*, 208, 224.
50. Pickstock, *After Writing*, 245.

in that which he emulates."⁵¹ And so, the Christian is brought to a fleeting moment of liturgical contemplation, and as receiving the Sabbath Queen, we see the "Face of the incarnate Logos."⁵² And we gaze upon the Messiah and time is changed.

Distinct from the humanisms, the ethics, and the politics for which others rightly hope, this is what the Sabbath uniquely offers: contemplation. Only the Sabbath can free Prometheus. For only in the Sabbath's liturgy are we are ushered tremulously into a different experience of time that is not only non-technological and humanizing but which ultimately brings us face to face with Christ. It is perhaps the only way we can remain human in the world of digital temporalities; it is the only way to salvation.

This then is the measure of our technologies. Do they help us inhabit what Fr. Harrison Ayre called the "sacramental worldview," seeing God in creation, everything in Christ, seeing all things from within Christ?⁵³ Or are we so rushed by our technologies that we forget ourselves, those closest to us, the poor, God? Has the devil given us these things? Are we "less assiduous in glorifying God" as we become increasingly dependent upon and addicted to the technologies that we use every day? Has the blue screen of the phone replaced the flickering votive of a night's quiet prayer?

Whatever may be collectively done, whatever is or isn't possible on some grander scale—for the Church, for parishes and communities and families—the mystery of the Sabbath must be lived together. All our efforts in ministry and discipline, our habits and hopes, must proceed from the understanding that this is what's at stake when it comes to technology. We cannot be indifferent, afford the conversation only shallow reflection or a few meaningless clichés designed to keep us in line as tame consumers and obedient users of technologies we have not spiritually discerned. The Church, Christians, must take up this spiritual work. In fact, a church that refused this task would—so Marcel figured—seem

---

51. Pickstock, *After Writing*, 208.
52. Pieper, *Happiness and Contemplation*, 108.
53. Ayre, *Mysterion*, 4.

"infected at its heart by a principle of falsehood and death."[54] It would be a zombie church, a technological and spiritual horror.

Which is why whatever we do and however technologically advanced or sophisticated we Christians may be, we must never forget to stop on the Sabbath. We must never think ourselves too busy to enter that different way of time and so rediscover ourselves in grace. For that is something we do not find when we log on but only when we sing with angels and archangels their unending hymn of praise.

---

54. Marcel, *Man against Mass Society*, 72.

Epilogue

SAINT AUGUSTINE BEGAN HIS *Confessions* with a simple fact: "our heart is unquiet until it rests in you." He ended it with a simple prayer for peace: "the peace that is repose, the peace of the Sabbath and the peace that knows no evening."[1] It knows no evening, this peaceful Sabbath, because it is God's Sabbath, a perfection in God that has only a morning, only a beginning, no setting sun. That is why so many of the fathers, as did Saint Gregory of Nyssa, suggest such blessedness is ceaseless desire.[2] "Joy will be fulfilled," Saint Bernard of Clairvaux said, "but there will be no end to desire, and therefore no end to the search."[3] Ended Eden is redeemed in an endless heavenly Jerusalem, happiness without horizon. That's the spiritual trajectory, the path the Sabbath opens.

What we've sought in this book—pure play, pure solidarity, pure contemplation—nears this Sabbath, opens to it, anticipates it. But to be clear, what is sought is not merely play or solidarity or contemplation but him in whom such things are found in their perfection. Our hearts are restless until they rest "in you," Saint Augustine wrote. That's an important detail. All of it—the ordering of our days, the interruptions and cessations of our commerce, work, technological pace, the worship of God Sunday by Sunday—constitutes a form of life formed to find Christ and not merely some abstract peace. Sunday matters, the Sabbath matters,

1. Augustine, *Confessions* 1.1.1; 13.35.50.
2. Gregory of Nyssa, *Life of Moses*, 233.
3. Bernard of Clairvaux, *Song of Songs* 84.1.2.

Epilogue

because since the exodus, that is what God's people have been looking for—God's rest and not just rest. That's what makes Christian talk of Sunday, or the weekend, more than talk about well-being and time management. That's what remains true about the Sunday Christ, the medieval image with which we began this book, however objectionable such an image may be for us today. The workaday details of our lives, the little things even, do in fact bear upon us spiritually. They bear upon us for good or for ill. There is nothing about our lives that is spiritually irrelevant, because the ordering of our lives is ultimately about finding God, about union with him. Every bit of our lives serves a spiritual purpose. We are still in the desert, at times just trying to survive, finding whatever is at hand to help. But all the while we are discovering too, little by little, that our survival is also our sanctification. Because God is with us sometimes as fire, sometimes in the tabernacle, sometimes with gifts of manna and water.

My hope, therefore, is that we, the people of God, simply keep going, that we remember we are still liberated exiles looking for home. Though we murmur, wander about in circles, foolishly cast idols, may we continue joyfully to remember to repent and retrace the path and renew our pilgrimage as often as we must. Weak creatures that we are, this will always be the case. In this little book I've pointed out only a few of the hazards of our pilgrimage; there are certainly more. May others help you find them; mind the path yourself. Whatever you do, however, never cease your pilgrimage, never stop looking for the Sabbath, searching for the Sunday Christ. For still he is searching for you.

Bibliography

Allen, Pauline, and Wendy Mayer. *John Chrysostom*. London: Routledge, 1999.

Alpert, Rebecca T. *Religion and Sports: An Introduction and Case Studies*. New York: Columbia University Press, 2015.

Alter, Adam. *Irresistible: The Rise of Addictive Technology and the Business of Keeping Us Hooked*. New York: Penguin, 2017.

Anderson, Gary A. *Charity: The Place of the Poor in the Biblical Tradition*. New Haven, CT: Yale University Press, 2013.

Ariès, Philippe. *Centuries of Childhood; a Social History of Family Life*. Translated by Robert Baldick. New York: Knopf, 1962.

Aristotle. *The Politics*. Translated by Ernest Barker. Oxford: Oxford University Press, 2009.

Aspen Institute Sports and Society Program. "Sport for All, Play for Life: A Playbook to Develop Every Student through Sports." https://www.aspeninstitute.org/wp-content/uploads/2015/01/Aspen-Institute-Project-Play-Report.pdf.

———. "Sport for All, Play for Life: A Playbook to Get Every Kid in the Game." https://www.aspeninstitute.org/wp-content/uploads/2022/02/FINAL-Aspen-Institute-Reimagining-School-Sports-playbook-pages.pdf.

———. "Research Brief: Sports Participation Rates among Underserved American Youth." https://www.aspeninstitute.org/wpcontent/uploads/files/content/docs/pubs/Project_Play_Underserved_Populations_Roundtable_Research_Brief.pdf.

———. "Youth Sports Facts: Challenges." https://www.aspenprojectplay.org/youth-sports/facts/challenges.

Augustine. *Concerning the City of God against the Pagans*. Translated by Henry Bettenson. London: Penguin, 1972.

———. *The Confessions*. Translated by Maria Boulding. Hyde Park: New City, 2001.

———. *Sermons for Christmas and Epiphany*. Translated by Thomas Comerford Lawler. Westminster: Newman, 1952.

Ayre, Harrison. *Mysterion: The Revelatory Power of the Sacramental Worldview*. Boston: Pauline, 2022.

Bibliography

Baker, William J. *Sports in the Western World*. Totowa, NJ: Rowman and Littlefield, 1982.
Basil. *On Social Justice*. Translated by C. Paul. Schroeder. Crestwood, NY: St. Vladimir's Seminary Press, 2009.
Barth, Karl. *Church Dogmatics*. 3/4. Edinburgh: T. & T. Clark, 2010.
Beer, Jeremy. *The Philanthropic Revolution: An Alternative History of American Charity*. Philadelphia: University of Pennsylvania Press, 2015.
Benedict XVI. *Caritas in Veritate*. In *Catholic Social Thought: Encyclicals and Documents from Pope Leo III to Pope Francis*, edited by David J. O'Brien and Thomas A. Shannon, 528–88. New York: Orbis, 2016.
Berdyaev, Nicholas. *The Bourgeois Mind*. Translated by Donald Attwater and Olga Bennigsen. Freeport: Books for Libraries, 1966.
Berlin, Isaiah. *Karl Marx: His Life and Environment*. Oxford: Oxford University Press, 1978.
Bernard of Clairvaux. *Song of Songs*. Translated by Kilian J. Walsh and Irene M. Edmonds. Kalamazoo: Cistercian, 1976.
Berry, Wendell. *Citizenship Papers*. Washington, DC: Shoemaker and Hoard, 2003.
Borgmann, Albert. *Power Failure: Christianity in the Culture of Technology*. Grand Rapids: Brazos, 2003.
———. *Technology and the Character of Contemporary Life: A Philosophical Inquiry*. Chicago: University of Chicago Press, 1984.
Bradshaw, Paul F., and Maxwell E. Johnson. *The Origins of Feasts, Fasts and Seasons in Early Christianity*. Collegeville, MN: Liturgical, 2011.
Brown, Peter. *Poverty and Leadership in the Later Roman Empire*. Hanover: University Press of New England, 2002.
———. *Through the Eye of a Needle: Wealth, the Fall of Rome, and the Making of Christianity in the West, 350–550 AD*. Princeton: Princeton University Press, 2012.
Campbell, Heidi, and Stephen Garner. *Networked Theology: Negotiating Faith in Digital Culture*. Grand Rapids: Baker, 2016.
"Can Youth Football Be Saved? (And Should It Be?)" *The Atlantic*, Nov. 15, 2013. https://www.theatlantic.com/entertainment/archive/2013/11/can-youth-football-be-saved-and-should-it-be/281536/.
Carr, Nicholas G. *The Shallows: What the Internet Is Doing to Our Brains*. New York: Norton, 2010.
Catechism of the Catholic Church. Vatican City: Libreria Editrice Vaticana, 2000.
Coeckelbergh, Mark. *Digital Technologies, Temporality, and the Politics of Co-Existence*. Cham, Switzerland: Palgrave Macmillan, 2022.
———. *Introduction to Philosophy of Technology*. New York: Oxford University Press, 2020.
Deleuze, Gilles. *Cinema: The Time-Image*. Minneapolis: University of Minnesota Press, 1986.
Dicastery for Laity, Family and Life. *Giving the Best of Yourself*. https://www.laityfamilylife.va/content/dam/laityfamilylife/Documenti/sport/dare-il-

Bibliography

meglio-di-se/060118%20ING%20-%20Dare%20il%20meglio%20di%20s%C3%A9%20-%20web.pdf.

Dichter, Ernest. *The Strategy of Desire*. Garden City, NY: Doubleday, 1960.

Dombrowski, Daniel A. "What Is Sport? What Should It Be?" In *Youth Sport and Spirituality: Catholic Perspectives*, edited by Patrick Kelly, 17–32. Notre Dame: University of Notre Dame Press, 2015.

Duffy, Eamon. *The Stripping of the Altars: Traditional Religion in England, 1400–1580*. New Haven, CT: Yale University Press, 2005.

Durkheim, Émile. *The Division of Labor in Society*. Translated by George Simpson. New York: Macmillan, 1933.

Ellul, Jacques. *Perspectives on Our Age: Jacques Ellul Speaks on His Life and Work*. Edited by Willem H. Vanderburg. New York: Seabury, 1981.

———. *The Presence of the Kingdom*. Colorado Springs: Helmers & Howard, 1989.

———. "The Technological Order." In *Philosophy and Technology*, edited by Carl Mitcham and Robert Macky, 86–105. New York: Free Press, 1983.

———. *The Technological Society*. New York: Knopf, 1964.

Endō, Shūsaku. *Silence: A Novel*. New York: Picador, 2016.

Farmer, Sharon. "From Personal Charity to Centralised Poor Relief: The Evolution of Responses to the Poor in Paris, c. 1250–1600." In *Experiences of Charity, 1250–1650*, edited by Anne M. Scott, 17–42. New York: Routledge, 2020.

Francis. *Laudato Si'*. In *Catholic Social Thought: Encyclicals and Documents from Pope Leo III to Pope Francis*, edited by David J. O'Brien and Thomas A. Shannon, 593–676. New York: Orbis, 2016.

———. *On Fraternity and Social Friendship (Fratelli Tutti)*. Vatican City: Libreria Editrice Vaticana, 2020.

Friedman, Hilary Levey. *Playing to Win: Raising Children in a Competitive Culture*. Berkeley: University of California Press, 2013.

———. "When Did Competitive Sports Take Over American Childhood?" *The Atlantic*, Sept. 20, 2013. https://www.theatlantic.com/education/archive/2013/09/when-did-competitive-sports-take-over-american-childhood/279868/.

Frischmann, Brett M., and Evan Selinger. *Re-Engineering Humanity*. Cambridge: Cambridge University Press, 2018.

Gaudium et Spes. In *Catholic Social Thought: Encyclicals and Documents from Pope Leo III to Pope Francis*, edited by David J. O'Brien and Thomas A. Shannon, 174–250. New York: Orbis, 2016.

Gehart, Diane. "Screening Screen Time: Evidence-Informed Guidelines for Parenting in the Digital Age." https://ftm.aamft.org/screening-screen-time-evidence-informed-guidelines-for-parenting-in-the-digital-age/.

Geremek, Bronisław. *Poverty: A History*. Oxford: Blackwell, 1994.

Goertz, Stephan. "Sport as a Sign of the Times." In *Sport and Christianity: A Sign of the Times in the Light of the Faith*, edited by Kevin Lixey et al., 189–205. Washington, DC: The Catholic University Press, 2012.

Bibliography

Grant, Robert M. *The Apostolic Fathers: A New Translation and Commentary*. Vol. 4: *Ignatius of Antioch*. Eugene, OR: Wipf & Stock, 2020.

Gregory of Nazianzus. *Select Orations*. Translated by Martha Vinson. Washington, DC: Catholic University of America Press, 2004.

Gregory of Nyssa. *The Life of Moses*. New York: Paulist, 1978.

Griffiths, Paul J. *Israel: A Christian Grammar*. Minneapolis: Fortress, 2023.

Guardini, Romano. *Letters from Lake Como: Explorations in Technology and the Human Race*. Translated by G. W. Bromiley. Grand Rapids: Eerdmans, 1994.

———. *The Spirit of the Liturgy*. Translated by Ada Lane. Mansfield Centre, CT: Martino, 2018.

Harrington, Michael. *The Other America: Poverty in the United States*. New York: Scribner, 1997.

Heschel, Abraham Joshua. *The Sabbath: Its Meaning for Modern Man*. New York: Farrar, Straus and Giroux, 1995.

Higgs, Robert J., and Michael Braswell. *An Unholy Alliance: The Sacred and Modern Sports*. Macon, GA: Mercer University Press, 2004.

Holman, Susan R. *The Hungry Are Dying: Beggars and Bishops in Roman Cappadocia*. New York: Oxford University Press, 2001.

Hoven, Matt, et al. *On the Eighth Day: A Catholic Theology of Sport*. Eugene, OR: Cascade, 2022.

Hughes, John. *The End of Work: Theological Critiques of Capitalism*. Malden, MA: Blackwell, 2007.

Huizinga, Johan. *Homo Ludens: A Study of the Play-Element in Culture*. Mansfield Centre, CT: Martino, 2014.

Huttenlocher, Daniel P., et al. *The Age of AI: And Our Human Future*. New York: Little, Brown, 2021.

Huxley, Aldous. *Brave New World*. San Francisco: Harper Perennial, 1998.

Illich, Ivan. *Tools for Conviviality*. 1st ed. New York: Harper & Row, 1973.

James, Samuel D. *Digital Liturgies: Rediscovering Christian Wisdom in an Online Age*. Wheaton: Crossway, 2023.

Jerome. *Select Letters*. Translated by F. A. Wright. Cambridge, MA: Harvard University Press, 1933.

John Chrysostom. *On Wealth and Poverty*. Translated by Catharine P. Roth. Crestwood, NY: St. Vladimir's Seminary Press, 1984.

John Paul II. *Dies Domini*. Chicago: Liturgy Training Publications, 1998.

———. *The Gospel of Life* (*Evangelium Vitae*). Vatican City: Libreria Editrice Vaticana, 1995.

———. *Laborem Exercens*. In *Catholic Social Thought: Encyclicals and Documents from Pope Leo III to Pope Francis*, edited by David J. O'Brien and Thomas A. Shannon, 380–423. New York: Orbis, 2016.

———. *On Social Concern (Sollicitudo rei socialis)*. In *Catholic Social Thought: Encyclicals and Documents from Pope Leo III to Pope Francis*, edited by David J. O'Brien and Thomas A. Shannon, 426–70. New York: Orbis, 2016.

———. *The Redeemer of Man (Redemptor Hominis)*. Boston: Pauline, 1979.

Bibliography

Johnson, Kelly S. *The Fear of Beggars: Stewardship and Poverty in Christian Ethics*. Grand Rapids: Eerdmans, 2007.

Keen, Sam. "The Development of the Idea of Being." In *The Philosophy of Gabriel Marcel*. La Salle, IL: Open Court, 1984.

Kelly, Patrick. "Christians and Sport: An Historical and Theological Overview." In *Youth Sport and Spirituality: Catholic Perspectives*, edited by Patrick Kelly, 33–61. Notre Dame: University of Notre Dame Press, 2015.

———. "Youth Sport and Spirituality." In *Youth Sport and Spirituality: Catholic Perspectives*, edited by Patrick Kelly, 133–54. Notre Dame: University of Notre Dame Press, 2015.

King, David, and Margot Starbuck. *Overplayed: A Parent's Guide to Sanity in the World of Youth Sports*. Harrisonburg: Herald, 2016.

King, Martin Luther, Jr. *A Knock at Midnight: Inspiration from the Great Sermons of Reverend Martin Luther King, Jr.* New York: Warner, 1998.

Koch, Alois. "Biblical and Patristic Foundations for Sport." In *Sport and Christianity: A Sign of the Times in the Light of the Faith*, edited by Kevin Lixey et al., 81–103. Washington, DC: The Catholic University Press, 2012.

Laband, David N., and Deborah Hendry Heinbuch. *Blue Laws: The History, Economics, and Politics of Sunday-Closing Laws*. Lexington: Lexington, 1987.

LeBaron, Genevieve. *Combatting Modern Slavery: Why Labour Governance Is Failing and What We Can Do About It*. Medford, MA: Polity, 2020.

Le Goff, Jacques. *History and Memory*. Translated by Steven Rendell and Elizabeth Claman. New York: Columbia University Press, 1992.

———. *Time, Work and Culture in the Middle Ages*. Translated by Arthur Goldhammer. Chicago: University of Chicago Press, 1980.

Leo XIII. *Rerum Novarum*. In *Catholic Social Thought: Encyclicals and Documents from Pope Leo III to Pope Francis*, edited by David J. O'Brien and Thomas A. Shannon, 14–40. New York: Orbis, 2016.

Lewis, C. S. *The Screwtape Letters*. New York: Harper One, 1996.

Lixey, Kevin. "Sport in the Magisterium of Pius XII." In *Sport and Christianity: A Sign of the Times in the Light of the Faith*, edited by Kevin Lixey et al., 104–20. Washington, DC: The Catholic University Press, 2012.

Lixey, Kevin, et al., eds. *Sport and Christianity: A Sign of the Times in the Light of the Faith*. Washington, DC: The Catholic University Press, 2012.

MacGillis, Alec. *Fulfillment: Winning and Losing in One-Click America*. New York: Farrar, Straus and Giroux, 2021.

MacIntyre, Alasdair. *After Virtue: A Study in Moral Theory*. Notre Dame: University of Notre Dame Press, 1984.

———. *Dependent Rational Animals: Why Human Beings Need the Virtues*. Chicago: Open Court, 1999.

MacKinnon, J. B. *The Day the World Stops Shopping: How Ending Consumerism Saves the Environment and Ourselves*. New York: Ecco, 2021.

Maddern, Philippa. "A Market for Charitable Performances? Bequests to the Poor and Their Recipients in Fifteenth-Century Norwich Wills." In

Bibliography

Experiences of Charity, 1250-1650, edited by Anne M. Scott, 79-104. New York: Routledge, 2020.

Maier, Bernhard. "Sport as a Pastoral Opportunity." In *Sport and Christianity: A Sign of the Times in the Light of the Faith*, edited by Kevin Lixey et al., 206-22. Washington, DC: The Catholic University Press, 2012.

Malesic, Jonathan. *The End of Burnout: Why Work Drains Us and How to Build Better Lives*. Oakland: University of California Press, 2022.

Marcel, Gabriel. *Man against Mass Society*. Translated by G. S. Fraser. South Bend, IN: St. Augustine's, 2008.

Maritain, Jacques. *Integral Humanism; Freedom in the Modern World; and, A Letter on Independence*. Vol. 11. Translated by Joseph W. Evans. Notre Dame: University of Notre Dame Press, 2012.

Maurin, Peter. *Easy Essays*. Chicago: Franciscan, 1984.

McCabe, Herbert. "Theology and Work—A Thomist View." In *Work: Christian Thought and Practice*, edited by John M. Todd, 211-21. London: Darton, Longman & Todd, 1960.

Misner, Paul. *Social Catholicism in Europe: From the Onset of Industrialization to the First World War*. New York: Crossroad, 1991.

Mollat, Michel. *The Poor in the Middle Ages: An Essay in Social History*. Translated by Arthur Goldhammer. New Haven, CT: Yale University Press, 1986.

Moschos, John. *The Spiritual Meadow*. Translated by John Wortley. Kalamazoo: Cistercian, 1992.

Mumford, Lewis. *The Myth of the Machine: The Pentagon of Power*. New York: Harcourt, Brace & World, 1970.

———. *The Myth of the Machine: Technics and Human Development*. New York: Harcourt, Brace & World, 1967.

———. *Technics and Civilization*. Chicago: University of Chicago Press, 2010.

———. "Technics and the Nature of Man." In *Philosophy and Technology*, edited by Carl Mitcham and Robert Macky, 77-85. New York: Free Press, 1983.

Musurillo, Herbert. *The Acts of the Christian Martyrs*. Oxford: Clarendon, 1972.

O'Connor, Flannery. *The Habit of Being: Letters*. New York: Farrar, Straus and Giroux, 1978.

Overman, Steven J. *The Protestant Ethic and the Spirit of American Sport: How Calvinism and Capitalism Shaped America's Games*. Macon, GA: Mercer University Press, 2011.

Pickstock, Catherine. *After Writing: On the Liturgical Consummation of Philosophy*. Oxford: Blackwell, 1998.

Pieper, Josef. *Happiness and Contemplation*. London: Burns & Oates, 1998.

———. *In Tune with the World: A Theory of Festivity*. South Bend, IN: St. Augustine's, 1999.

———. *Leisure: The Basis of Culture*. San Francisco: Ignatius, 2009.

Plato. *Phaedrus*. Translated by W. C. Helmbold and W. G. Rabinowitz. Indianapolis: Bobbs-Merrill, 1956.

Bibliography

———. *Protagoras*. Translated by Stanley Lombardo and Karen Bell. Indianapolis: Hackett, 1992.

Postman, Neil. *The Disappearance of Childhood*. New York: Delacorte, 1982.

———. *Technopoly: The Surrender of Culture to Technology*. New York: Knopf, 1992.

Power, Clark. "Playing Like a Champion Today: Youth Sport and Moral Development." In *Youth Sport and Spirituality: Catholic Perspectives*, edited by Patrick Kelly, 88–110. Notre Dame: University of Notre Dame Press, 2015.

Press, Eyal. *Dirty Work: Essential Jobs and the Hidden Toll of Inequality in America*. New York: Farrar, Straus and Giroux, 2021.

Price, Joseph L., ed. *From Season to Season: Sports as American Religion*. Macon, GA: Mercer University Press, 2001.

Rahner, Hugo. *Man at Play*. Translated by Brian Battershaw and Edward Quinn. Providence: Cluny, 2019.

Ratzinger, Joseph. *Behold the Pierced One: An Approach to a Spiritual Christology*. Translated by Graham Harrison. San Francisco: Ignatius, 1986.

Ratzinger, Joseph, and Peter Seewald. *Salt of the Earth*. Translated by Adrian Walker. San Francisco: Ignatius, 1997.

Reeves, Richard V. *Dream Hoarders: How the American Upper Middle Class Is Leaving Everyone Else in the Dust, Why That Is a Problem, and What to Do about It*. Washington, DC: Brookings Institution, 2017.

Reiss, Athene. *The Sunday Christ: Sabbatarianism in English Medieval Wall Painting*. Oxford: Archaeopress, 2000.

The Religion of Sports. https://www.religionofsports.com/.

Ripatrazone, Nick. *Digital Communion: Marshall McLuhan's Spiritual Vision for a Virtual Age*. Minneapolis: Fortress, 2022.

Rowlands, Anna. *Towards a Politics of Communion: Catholic Social Teaching in Dark Times*. London: T. & T. Clark, 2022.

Rubin, Miri. *Charity and Community in Medieval Cambridge*. Cambridge: Cambridge University Press, 1987.

Sacrosanctum Concilium. In *Vatican Council II: The Conciliar and Post Conciliar Documents*, edited by Austin Flannery, 1–36. New York: Costello, 1998.

Shakespeare, William. *Antony and Cleopatra*. New York: Washington Square, 1999.

Shields, David Light, and Brenda Light Bredemeier. "Reclaiming Competition in Youth Sports." In *Youth Sport and Spirituality: Catholic Perspectives*, edited by Patrick Kelly, 111–32. Notre Dame: University of Notre Dame Press, 2015.

Shulevitz, Judith. *The Sabbath World: Glimpses of a Different Order of Time*. New York: Random House, 2011.

Spadaro, Antonio. *Cybertheology: Thinking Christianity in the Era of the Internet*. Translated by Mari Way. New York: Fordham University Press, 2014.

Soto, Domingo de. *Deliberation on the Cause of the Poor*. Grand Rapids: CLP Academic, 2022.

Bibliography

Solomon, Jon. "Injury Treatments Are Suspended Due to Public Health Needs." Project Play, Mar. 24, 2020. https://projectplay.org/news/2020/3/24/injury-treatments-are-suspended-due-to-public-health-needs.

Steiner-Adair, Catherine. *The Big Disconnect: Protecting Childhood and Family Relationships in the Digital Age.* New York: Harper, 2014.

Taylor, Charles. *The Language Animal: The Full Shape of the Human Linguistic Capacity.* Cambridge, MA: Belknap, 2016.

Tertullian. *Apologeticus.* Translated by Alex Souter. Cambridge: Cambridge University Press, 2012.

Thomas Aquinas. "Prologue to the Commentary on Boethius' *De Hebdomadibus.*" In *Albert and Thomas: Selected Writings*, edited by Simon Tugwell, 527–28. New York: Paulist, 1988.

———. *Summa Theologiae: Prima Secundae, 1–70.* Lander, WY: Aquinas Institute 2012.

Thompson, Derek. "American Meritocracy Is Killing Youth Sports." *The Atlantic*, Nov. 6, 2018. https://www.theatlantic.com/ideas/archive/2018/11/income-inequality-explains-decline-youth-sports/574975/.

———. *On Work: Money, Meaning, Identity.* New York: Zando, 2023.

Turkle, Sherry. *Alone Together: Why We Expect More from Technology and Less from Each Other.* New York: Basic, 2011.

Vallor, Shannon. *Technology and the Virtues: A Philosophical Guide to a Future Worth Wanting.* Oxford: Oxford University Press, 2018.

Vitry, Jacques de. *The Exempla.* London: The Folk-Lore Society, 1890.

Weber, Max. *The Protestant Ethic and the Spirit of Capitalism.* Translated by Talcott Parsons. London: Routledge, 2001.

Weil, Simone. *Gravity and Grace.* Translated by Arthur Wills. Lincoln: University of Nebraska Press, 1997.

Zweig, Stefan. *The World of Yesterday.* Translated by Benjamin H. Huebsch and Helmut Ripperger. Lincoln: University of Nebraska Press, 2013.

www.ingramcontent.com/pod-product-compliance
Lightning Source LLC
Chambersburg PA
CBHW031343160426
43196CB00007B/718